P9-BYM-898

STORIES IN HISTORY

THE STRUGGLE FOR
CIVIL RIGHTS

1940s–1970s

nextext

Printed in China.

ISBN-13: 978-0-618-22208-7
ISBN-10: 0-618-22208-1

6 7 8 9 NPC 09 08 07 06

Table of Contents

In 1939, famous African-American singer Marian Anderson was denied the use of a concert hall in Washington, D.C. Then First Lady Eleanor Roosevelt took action.

To protest racism in the military and defense industries, African-American labor leader A. Philip Randolph organizes a huge march on Washington, D.C. But President Franklin Roosevelt tries to get Randolph to call it off.

PART 2: THE CIVIL RIGHTS MOVEMENT

PART 3: A CHANGING SOCIETY

About this Book

The stories are historical fiction. They are based on historical fact, but some of the characters and events may be fictional. In the Sources section, you'll learn which is which, and where the information came from.

The illustrations are all historical. If they are from a time different from the story, the caption tells you. Original documents help you understand the time period. Maps let you know where things were.

Items explained in People and Terms to Know are repeated in the Glossary. Look there if you come across a name or term you don't know.

Historians do not always know or agree on the exact dates of events in the past. The letter c before a date means "about" (from the Latin word circa).

If you would like to read more about these exciting times, you will find recommendations in Reading on Your Own.

A protest marcher rests her muddy feet after marching from Selma to Montgomery, Alabama. ▶

Background

"Keep your eyes on the prize, Hold on."

—African-American spiritual
adapted by civil rights workers

Segregated America

"Get your rights, Jack!"
—song sung by civil rights workers in the South

Slavery ended in 1865, but equality for African Americans was still a long way off. Discrimination was legal in the United States well into the 20th century. Laws as well as customs kept the races apart. And almost all white people believed they were superior to people of other races. Their actions showed this belief in every part of community life.

Jim Crow Laws

A series of laws in most Southern states until the 1950s kept blacks and whites apart. They are called Jim Crow laws. These laws required separate schools, separate restaurants, and even separate water fountains for whites and blacks. A town might have two schools, for instance—one for whites and one for blacks. The all-black school was never as good as the "whites-only" one.

Many Groups Treated Unfairly

Groups of people other than African Americans were also targets of unfair laws and discrimination.

During the Second World War, for example, after Japan attacked the United States, the U.S. government took many Japanese Americans from their homes and forced them to live in prison camps. The government said it was worried that they might be on Japan's side, but the real reason was probably racial prejudice. The United States also fought against Italy and Germany in this war, but it did not put Italian Americans and German Americans in camps.

▲

Blacks and whites wait in separate parts of a bus station in Memphis, Tennessee, in 1943.

There were other cultural groups who faced prejudice in the United States. Latino Americans spoke a different language, and their culture was unfamiliar to white Americans. The same was true of Native Americans, who had a hard time finding jobs and homes where they wanted.

Racial Violence

There were many laws that kept whites apart from other races. But laws did not do the job alone. Violence also played a part. Whites sometimes threatened to hurt African Americans who broke the Jim Crow laws. In an act called lynching, white mobs murdered African Americans accused of some crime. In some cases, African Americans were lynched even when they did not break the law. A black person could be lynched just for showing disrespect to a white person.

Race riots were another form of violence against people of color. In these riots, angry white mobs attacked members of other races. In 1943, for instance, there were riots in Alabama, Texas, New York, California, and several other states. The riots sometimes scared people of color into accepting the way things were.

The Beginning of Change

By 1954, laws still kept people of different races apart, and racial prejudice remained common. Yet, some things had already begun to change:

1942

The Congress of Racial Equality, a group working for fairness for all races, is founded.

1943

Chinese immigrants are allowed into the United States once again.

1947

Jackie Robinson joins the Brooklyn Dodgers and breaks major league baseball's "color line."

1948

President Harry Truman tells the military to stop keeping blacks and whites apart.

1954

The U.S. Supreme Court rules that "whites-only" schools are against the Constitution.

Over the next 20 years, more changes would occur. They would come much faster, too, as more groups struggled to enjoy basic civil and economic rights.

Outside the Supreme Court, the lawyers who had successfully argued the 1954 case against separate schools are celebrating. Thurgood Marshall (middle) would later become a Supreme Court Justice.

The Civil Rights Movement

"My feets is tired, but my soul is rested."

—woman who took part in the
Montgomery bus boycott

After the Supreme Court's ruling in 1954 that "whites-only" schools were not legal, people in the South started to protest the way things were. The first large protest began in December 1955. In Montgomery, Alabama, a woman named Rosa Parks refused to give up her seat in the "whites-only" section of a city bus. She was arrested.

The Bus Boycott

To protest the segregated buses, African Americans in Montgomery organized a boycott of the city bus line. For many weeks, no black person in Montgomery rode the bus. Instead, they walked or carpooled. The bus company lost money but still would not change its ways. It was almost a year after the boycott began when the Supreme Court said that the bus company could not have "whites-only" seats. The protesters had won, and the boycott was called off.

Schools

The schools soon became another battleground during the 1950s. In several Southern cities, African-American students began to attend schools that had been "whites-only." It was not easy for them. In Little Rock, Arkansas, angry white mobs threatened nine black students who wanted to attend formerly all-white Central High School in 1957. The U.S. Army had to protect the students so they could go to school.

Other Protests

Protests quickly became more common. Groups of African-American students began to enter "whites-only" restaurants. They sat at the tables and refused to leave during these "sit-ins." Instead, they waited peacefully to be served. Sometimes the students were beaten up or sent to jail. But by late 1960, some of the restaurants were serving blacks along with whites.

The same thing took place on inter-city buses in the South. African-American "Freedom Riders" tried to board the buses. Some were beaten up. One was paralyzed. But in the end the Freedom Riders got the buses to take them where they wanted to go.

Young African-American men stage a sit-in at a "whites only" lunch counter in Greensboro, North Carolina, in 1960.

The March on Washington

In August 1963, civil rights leaders planned a march on Washington. This was a large and peaceful protest. About a quarter of a million people came from all over the country. Many of them rode special buses and trains. The march was a huge success, especially since people of all races marched side by side.

The marchers at Washington asked Congress to pass laws that would help African Americans in the South. Some of the laws were passed in 1964.

Growth in Voter Registration

Percentage of Mississippi blacks registered to vote:

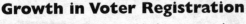

1964

7%

1968

59%

Others were passed the following year. The laws made it easier for African Americans to vote and made it harder for the states to keep the races apart.

Civil Rights in the North

In the late 1960s the Civil Rights movement began to look at the situation in the North as well as the South. Many African Americans had left the South to live in the large cities of the North. The North did not have laws to keep the races apart. Still, things were not good for many African Americans in Northern cities. Most Northern blacks were quite poor. They faced prejudice in housing, jobs, and education.

Anger Builds

By this time, many African Americans and their supporters were angered by how slowly things were changing. Even after years of work, millions of African Americans still lived in poverty. There was still prejudice, and there was still violence. To some people it seemed that things were never going to get better.

Changing Leadership

This growing anger affected the leadership of the Civil Rights movement. From the time of the Montgomery bus boycott, African-American civil rights leaders, such as Rev. Martin Luther King, Jr., had stressed nonviolent protest. They had worked with whites toward the goal of an integrated society.

As African-American anger grew, new leaders came forward. The most powerful of these new leaders was Malcolm X. Unlike Martin Luther King, Malcolm X believed in separating blacks from whites. Malcolm X also believed that African Americans should reach their goals "by any means necessary"—including violence. Shortly before he was assassinated in 1965, Malcolm X changed his views. He began to picture a world where all races could live in peace. But he had little time to spread his new message.

Black Power

By 1966, a new movement called Black Power had begun. "Black Power" became the slogan of African Americans who agreed that nonviolent protest could not solve their problems. They were willing to fight back if beaten or attacked. These men and women also worked to help African Americans improve their self-image. They taught and studied black history and culture as well.

▲ Student civil rights leader Stokely Carmichael speaks at a conference held by Students for a Democratic Society (SDS) on the Berkeley campus of the University of California in the late 1960s.

A Changing Society

"Viva la huelga!" ["Long live the strike!"]
—rallying cry of Mexican-American
migrant workers

African Americans were not the only people of color to work for civil rights. Many other groups also fought for change during the 1950s and 1960s. Latinos, Asian Americans, and Native Americans all won new rights at this time too.

Migrant Workers

Latino Americans worked especially hard for basic rights during the 1960s. Many Mexican Americans in the United States lived and worked in California and the states of the Southwest. They were migrant workers—fruit and vegetable pickers who traveled from farm to farm. They were poorly paid and poorly treated. In 1962, migrant workers formed an organization called the United Farm Workers Association. This union helped the workers bargain for more money and better living conditions.

▲
Cesar Chavez works with his wife Helen during a farm labor strike
in Delano, California.

But many farmers did not accept the union. Some farmers refused to work with pickers who joined it. Others beat up union leaders who came to talk to the workers. In 1965, union migrant workers went on strike and refused to pick grapes. The following year, union leader Cesar Chavez led a march to the California state capital to protest migrants' living and working conditions. About 10,000 people joined the protest.

Civil Rights Victories

Native Americans also struggled for their rights during these years. In 1973, a group called the American Indian Movement took over a South Dakota village called Wounded Knee. This protest helped make the problems of Native Americans known to the general public.

The protests and the changes of the Civil Rights Era have had a huge effect for people of color in the United States. Once, they were pushed aside by prejudice and unfair laws. Today, the laws are much fairer. In many ways, there is less prejudice, too. People from many different backgrounds are also much more aware of their culture and history than they used to be.

Multicultural America

The civil rights movements had an important effect on all of America. The United States today is a more multicultural place than it ever was before. This means that groups from many ethnic backgrounds have brought their cultures to the United States. American art, literature, and music

▲
Leaders of the American Indian Movement at Wounded Knee in 1973.

Civil Rights Protests, Marches, and Struggles

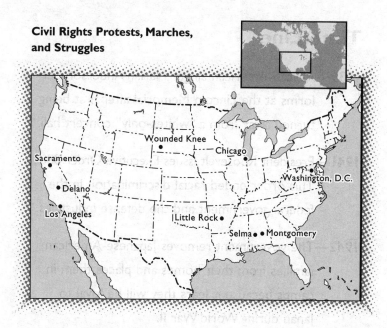

have all been influenced. People of color now live in places that used to be for "whites-only." More and more, political power is shared among different racial and cultural groups. Multicultural America is here to stay.

Time Line

1939—African-American singer Marian Anderson performs at the Lincoln Memorial after first being turned away from a "whites-only" concert hall.

1941—President Roosevelt issues Executive Order 8802. This order ended racial discrimination in the federal government and the defense industries.

1942—The government removes Japanese-American families from their homes and places them in camps because it fears they will be loyal to Japan during World War II.

1943—In Los Angeles, white mobs attack Mexican-American neighborhoods in the Zoot Suit Riots.

1947—Jackie Robinson breaks the major league baseball "color line."

1948—President Truman orders that the military no longer separate black and white soldiers.

1954—The Supreme Court's decision in *Brown v. Board of Education of Topeka* outlaws one-race public schools.

1955—The Montgomery bus boycott begins.

1956—The U.S. Supreme Court rules against the segregation of Montgomery buses.

1957—Little Rock, Arkansas, schools are desegregated.

1960—Sit-ins at restaurants and lunch counters occur across the South.

1961—"Freedom rides" take place on buses in the South.

1962—The National Farm Workers Association is founded.

1963—Martin Luther King, Jr., delivers "I Have a Dream" speech at the March on Washington.

1964—The Civil Rights Act is passed.

1965—Malcolm X is assassinated; the Voting Rights Act of 1965 is passed; farm workers begin strike against grape growers.

1968—Martin Luther King, Jr., is assassinated; there is widespread rioting in U.S. cities; the American Indian Movement is founded.

1973—Native American protesters take over Wounded Knee, South Dakota.

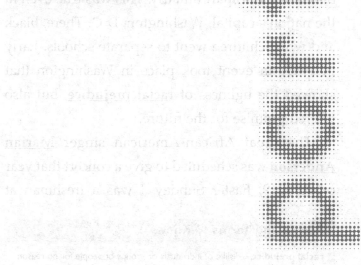

Segregated America

Marian Anderson Sings at the Lincoln Memorial

BY FITZGERALD HIGGINS

In the 1930s, much of America had laws that kept different races apart unfairly. This was true even in the nation's capital, Washington, D.C. There, black and white children went to separate schools. Early in 1939, an event took place in Washington that showed the ugliness of **racial prejudice**, but also offered promise for the future.

The great African-American singer **Marian Anderson** was scheduled to give a concert that year on April 9, Easter Sunday. I was a freshman at

---

People and Terms to Know

racial prejudice—dislike of individuals or groups of people for no reason other than their skin color or race; belief that people of racial groups other than one's own are inferior.

Marian Anderson—(1897–1993) famous singer who was the first African American to perform at the Metropolitan Opera.

Marian Anderson sings at the Lincoln Memorial.

Howard University at the time. Anderson had come every year for the past three years to sing a concert at Howard. I loved music, and I really loved opera singing. I couldn't wait to hear her sing. This year, Howard University wanted to hold Anderson's concert in a very fine local auditorium, Constitution Hall.

Constitution Hall was owned by a well-known group of patriotic women, the **Daughters of the American Revolution**, or DAR. The people organizing the concert asked the DAR if Anderson could perform in their hall. The DAR refused, saying that they had a rule that performers at Constitution Hall had to be "white artists only."

The DAR's refusal upset a lot of people. One of these was **Eleanor Roosevelt**, wife of President Franklin D. Roosevelt. The **first lady** was a member

---

People and Terms to Know

Howard University—college founded in Washington, D.C., in 1867 and dedicated to the education of African Americans.

Daughters of the American Revolution—patriotic organization founded in 1890. Its members are women whose families supported the American Revolution.

Eleanor Roosevelt—(1884–1962) first lady of the United States (1933–1945), writer, and American diplomat; wife of President Franklin Roosevelt.

first lady—wife of the chief executive of a country, state, or city.

of the DAR, and on February 26, she wrote a letter to its head. In it, she said she would no longer be part of the DAR. She explained that she was "in complete disagreement with the attitude taken in refusing Constitution Hall to a great artist." The first lady went on to say, "You had an opportunity to lead in an enlightened way and it seems to me your organization has failed."

Beginning in 1936, Mrs. Roosevelt had written a daily newspaper column known as "My Day." On the day after she left the DAR, the first lady used her column to explain her reasons. She never mentioned the DAR by name. Instead, she asked a general moral question: What do you do when you belong

"You had an opportunity to lead in an enlightened way and it seems to me your organization has failed."

to a group but disapprove of its actions? Do you leave it in anger or try to improve it by working from within?

Very soon, people across the country knew what organization Mrs. Roosevelt was talking about and what she had decided to do. In general, the American public supported her decision to resign from the DAR. In a national survey taken two weeks later, 67 percent of the country approved of her choice. The exception was the South, where a majority disagreed with her decision. But some Southerners said they had no objection to Marian Anderson performing in Constitution Hall. They just didn't like the first lady "making a fuss about it."

Another person who responded to the DAR's refusal was Walter White, an official of the **NAACP**. One of Anderson's supporters had suggested that the singer perform outdoors in the small park across the street from Constitution Hall. White didn't like this idea very much. He said, "I think it would be undignified and too much like a small boy

---

People and Terms to Know

NAACP—National Association for the Advancement of Colored People, organization founded in 1909 to advance the legal and political rights of African Americans.

thumbing his nose at the back of a larger boy who has beaten him up."

I'm a small fellow myself. I knew what it was like to want to thumb my nose at larger boys. But I could see White's point. Instead, he suggested a bold new idea. Marian Anderson would perform outside, but at the **Lincoln Memorial**. A concert by an African-American performer held at the Lincoln Memorial would be a powerful statement for racial justice. But to perform there, Anderson still needed permission. Use of the Lincoln Memorial was controlled by the **Interior Department**. Walter White wrote a friend of his who was Assistant Secretary of the Interior.

White's friend soon talked to his boss, Harold Ickes, **Secretary of the Interior**. Ickes, in turn, talked to his boss, President Franklin Roosevelt. All of them were pleased with the idea of Marian Anderson performing outside at the Lincoln Memorial. President Roosevelt told Secretary Ickes

---

People and Terms to Know

Lincoln Memorial—huge, temple-like monument to President Abraham Lincoln in Washington, D.C.

Interior Department—department in the U.S. government that protects public lands and natural resources. It has responsibility for national parks and monuments such as the Lincoln Memorial.

Secretary of the Interior—head of the Interior Department. "Secretary" is the title given to the head of any such government department that reports directly to the president.

to do everything he could to make sure the concert was a big success. On March 30, the Secretary of the Interior announced that Marian Anderson would sing at the Lincoln Memorial. The stage was set.

Meanwhile, how did Marian Anderson feel about everything that was happening?

The singer was on tour elsewhere while those who planned her concert dealt with the DAR. She said later she understood how important this concert had become only after seeing the headline on a San Francisco newspaper: MRS. ROOSEVELT TAKES STAND. RESIGNS FROM D.A.R.

Anderson felt that she was carrying a burden. It was not one she enjoyed.

As the days went by and the date of her Easter Sunday concert approached, Anderson felt that she was carrying a burden. It was not one she enjoyed. Instead of being simply about fine music, her concert was now about racial equality.

On the night before the concert, she couldn't sleep. By midnight, she felt so frightened that she called one of the concert organizers and asked if she really had to sing. But by the next morning, she was ready.

Easter Sunday morning in Washington that year was unusually cold and gray. Anderson's concert was to take place at five in the afternoon. By that time, a huge crowd had gathered in front of the Lincoln Memorial. The Park Service later estimated that there were 75,000 people present. Most of us were African Americans, but there were plenty of white people there too. We had been afraid that racists might make trouble, but everything was very peaceful as we waited for the concert to begin.

The sun began to shine a bit, but it was still cold. I watched Marian Anderson walk up to the bank of six microphones at the front of the platform. I could see that she was pulling her fur coat tightly around her shoulders. She may have been cold, or perhaps just nervous. I couldn't blame her if she was. Facing that huge, hushed waiting crowd, she looked very small and alone.

Then she began to sing "My Country, 'Tis of Thee." It was like I had never heard the song before. The hair stood up on the back of my neck. I felt suddenly that this country really did belong to all of us, not just those folks whose ancestors had come over on the _Mayflower_.

People and Terms to Know

Mayflower—ship that brought English settlers to Massachusetts in 1620.

▲
A huge crowd gathers to hear Marian Anderson's concert on April 9, 1939.

Marian Anderson sang for about half an hour. When she finished, the audience clapped and clapped. We wanted her to keep singing, her voice was so beautiful. Then she came back to the microphone and sang the spiritual "Nobody Knows the Trouble I've Seen." Afterwards she thanked us all for coming to hear her sing. I still remember her words: "I can't tell you what you have done for me today. I thank you from the bottom of my heart."

What *we* had done for her?

The real question was, what had she done for all of us? Well, she'd given us pride in ourselves as African Americans and hope for our country's future. I no longer felt like such a little fellow. I looked at the huge statue of Abraham Lincoln, the president who had freed the slaves. I felt as big as it was, bigger even! Suddenly I knew why people had wanted the concert at the Lincoln Memorial. Lincoln had offered hope to our people 80 years ago, and now Marian Anderson's performance offered hope of a different kind.

Walter White, when he later wrote about the concert, best captured what Marian Anderson did for us that day. After the concert was over, he noticed a thin, very dressed-up black girl in the audience. She didn't look like the type who attended many concerts like this one—maybe because her hands showed that she worked hard for a living. Although she was some distance from Marian Anderson, she was reaching out with these work-worn hands, as if trying to touch her. Here is how White described her:

"Tears streamed down the girl's dark face. Her hat was askew but in her eyes flamed hope bordering on ecstasy. Life which had been none too easy for her now held out greater hope because one who was also colored and who, like herself, had known poverty, privation, and prejudice, had, by her genius, gone a long way toward conquering **bigotry**. If Marian Anderson could do it, the girl's eyes seemed to say, then I can too."

> "Tears streamed down the girl's dark face. Her hat was askew but in her eyes flamed hope bordering on ecstasy."

QUESTIONS TO CONSIDER

1. Why do you think the Daughters of the American Revolution refused to permit Marian Anderson to sing at Constitution Hall?

2. Why did Anderson's supporters want her to sing at the Lincoln Memorial?

3. What message did Walter White think that the young black girl gained from Marian Anderson's concert?

4. If you were a member of an organization that did something you disapproved of, how would you respond?

People and Terms to Know

bigotry (BIGH•uh•tree)—prejudice against people of other races, religions, or backgrounds.

Feb. 26, 1939.

My dear Mrs. Henry Robert, Jr.:

I am afraid that I have never been a very useful member of the Daughters of the American Revolution, so I know it will make very little difference to you whether I resign, or whether I continue to be a member of your organization.

However, I am in complete disagreement with the attitude taken in refusing Constitution Hall to a great artist. You have set an example which seems to me unfortunate, and I feel obligated to send you my resignation. You had an opportunity to lead in an enlightened way and it seems to me that your organization has failed.

I realize that many people will not agree with me, but feeling as I do this seems to me the only proper procedure to follow.

Very sincerely yours,
Eleanor Roosevelt

A. Philip Randolph Threatens a March

BY WALTER HAZEN

I knew **A. Philip Randolph** from way back—so far back that I even got away with calling him "Asa" (his first name) once in a while. You see, he preferred to be called Philip. Anyway, back in 1911, we met when we were working as waiters on the same steamship. We were both young, and I considered us lucky to have good, steady jobs.

But things weren't good enough for Philip. He tried to organize us waiters in a protest against the working conditions. Well, that was Philip from the start. Here he was barely out of his teens, and he

---

People and Terms to Know

A. Philip Randolph—Asa Philip Randolph (1889–1979), African-American labor leader. His threat of a march on Washington by black Americans in 1941 led President Franklin D. Roosevelt to issue an order ending discrimination in the defense industries.

An African-American man works alongside whites to build a wing panel for an airplane at North American Aviation in October 1942.

was already trying to get black Americans to band together to improve their quality of life.

In private, I agreed with him. In front of the bosses, though, I kept my mouth shut. Philip was right: there was a lot about the job that could have been better. But I felt I couldn't risk losing it. You see, I thought about my father's life down on the farm in Georgia. I thought about going back to work in the dirt and the blazing sun. I thought about always being worried about keeping enough money for myself to be able to eat. No, sir, that wasn't for me.

I guess it might have been easier to speak openly about prejudice in Harlem than in Florida.

Philip didn't mind taking risks, though. And as a reward for trying to protest, he was fired. Could be that the bosses figured that firing Philip would make him change his ways, but the truth was, it only fired him up.

He was the son of a minister and grew up in Jacksonville, Florida. When he was 22, he moved to the Harlem district of New York City. There he met and talked with people who saw the wrong things going on and cared deeply about trying to right them. I guess it might have been easier to speak openly about prejudice in Harlem than in Florida. In

Harlem, a community of black writers, poets, and artists were making people hear their concerns.

In 1925, Philip and I crossed paths again. I had been working in the railroad industry for five years. I liked dry land better, and I liked the pay better too. Still, there was room for improvement in the working conditions and—you guessed it—that's where Philip stepped in. He got everyone together who had a job like mine and formed the **Brotherhood of Sleeping Car Porters**. Now we were a union of workers. We couldn't just be fired (like Philip on the steamship) if we voiced our concerns. White men had had unions for years and years, but this was kind of a first for black men.

Like myself, Philip was moved by the writings of **W.E.B. Du Bois**. Du Bois believed that blacks should educate themselves as much as possible and fight for their civil rights. Philip agreed. He felt that

---

People and Terms to Know

Brotherhood of Sleeping Car Porters—first largely black modern labor union in America. It represented porters, workers who carried loads and baggage on railroad sleeping cars.

W.E.B. Du Bois (doo•BOYS)—(1868–1963) African-American historian and writer. He helped found the National Association for the Advancement of Colored People in 1909.

too many blacks were satisfied with simply learning a trade and "getting along" with white people.

Philip's work with the Brotherhood of Sleeping Car Porters made him nationally known. In the 1930s, he led the fight to end discrimination in industry and the armed forces. I had a teenage son who was interested in serving in the military—I guess he saw it as a step up from my job the same way I had tried to improve over my father's. So we followed Philip's progress, with my son Michael always wanting to hear stories about the great Mr. Randolph back when we were both waiters.

▲
A. Philip Randolph stands (front row, dark coat) with a group of railroad employees in Washington, D.C.

Michael and I weren't the only ones following Philip's career and ideas. His views caught the attention of Eleanor Roosevelt, the wife of the president. She mentioned him to her husband, and the president invited him and other black leaders to a conference at the White House on September 27, 1940. The purpose of the conference was to discuss the concerns of black Americans.

In a letter, Philip told me before he went to Washington that he planned to ask the president to end segregation in the armed forces.

"Do you think the president will agree?" I asked Michael after Philip had departed for the capital.

"Not a chance, Dad," Michael replied, angry. "Would white soldiers from the South sleep in the same barracks with black soldiers? They won't even even drink out of the same water fountains! Will they obey black officers? I don't think so."

"Yeah," I sighed. "Roosevelt isn't going to upset Southerners in Congress. He needs their votes to get his programs across."

It turned out we were right. The president did not agree to end segregation in the armed forces. To make matters worse, one of his aides said later that Philip and the others approved of the policy! Philip was furious. This was an out-and-out lie. From that moment on, Philip knew that more direct action was needed if the problems of America's blacks were to be heard.

A few months after his meeting with the president, Philip hit on a plan. It came to him while he was traveling by train through the South. Looking out the train's windows at cabins where **sharecroppers** lived, he got an idea. It's funny, but he could have been looking at where my Dad worked for all I know.

"I think we ought to get 10,000 Negroes to march on Washington in protest— march down Pennsylvania Avenue."

Anyway, Philip turned to a friend and said: "I think we ought to get 10,000 Negroes to march on Washington in protest—march down Pennsylvania Avenue." The idea was to do things in a peaceful way, but in a way that showed how many people were affected by racism. What better way to attract attention to the problems of black Americans than a mass march on Washington, D.C., the nation's capital?

People and Terms to Know

sharecroppers—farmers who do not own land but grow crops for the owners in exchange for some of the harvest.

When I heard about Philip's plan, I thought of **Mahatma Gandhi** in India. Gandhi used nonviolent methods to gain the freedom and rights of his people. That meant not losing your cool, no matter how upset you make the other side. The watching world then sees that your demands are reasonable, and that you aren't just out to make trouble.

Philip set the date for the march at July 1, 1941. He and others then founded the March on Washington Movement to plan and direct the event. Philip explained his decision to organize a march by saying, "In this period of power politics, nothing counts but pressure, more pressure, and still more pressure."

The demonstration was to be nonviolent. No laws would be broken and no property destroyed. White supporters, although they were encouraged to cheer the marchers along, would not be allowed to participate.

"There are some things Negroes must do alone," Philip explained.

People and Terms to Know

Mahatma Gandhi (GAHN•dee)—(1869–1948) Mohandas Karamchand Gandhi led India to independence from Great Britain in 1947 after years of nonviolent protests. His supporters called him *Mahatma*, meaning "great soul."

By May 1941, enthusiasm for the march was growing. Support came from blacks throughout the country. African-American church groups, women's clubs, and other organizations began raising money to travel to Washington. Philip himself made the rounds of Harlem shops and businesses promoting the march. My job kept me from attending the march, but Michael planned on going with my brother, who lives in Virginia. Everything was going as planned.

He feared that the marchers would be seriously hurt even if they themselves were not violent.

And that's what worried the president. He feared that the marchers would be seriously hurt even if they themselves were not violent. He was also afraid that other groups would try the same thing, so that the capital would have to deal with march after march. Roosevelt hoped Philip would change his mind. He had federal officials send a letter to defense industry companies asking them to make a better effort to hire blacks.

Well, Philip's never going to agree to that, I thought.

And he didn't. Realizing that Philip meant business, the president invited him to the White House a second time on June 18, 1941. Once again, he asked Philip to call off the march. Philip refused. He told the president that only an **executive order** ending discrimination in the defense industry would make him cancel the demonstration.

Faced with such determination, the president gave in. One week later he issued Executive Order 8802. This order ended discrimination in the federal government and the defense industries. It also set up the **Fair Employment Practices Committee**.

In a sense, Philip and all black Americans had won. Maybe it was just one small battle in a struggle that would take decades, but it was still something. Although segregation did not end in the armed forces until seven years later, the first of Philip's goals had been met. Reaching the other goals was only a matter of time.

What happened to my son, Michael? Well, he's retired now, like me. The difference is, he retired a colonel in the U.S. Army.

People and Terms to Know

executive order—rule made by the president that has the force of law.
Fair Employment Practices Committee—government agency established to prevent discrimination against blacks in the defense industries.

1. What was the Brotherhood of Sleeping Car Porters?

2. Why did Randolph plan a march on Washington, D.C.?

3. Why was planning a march an effective way of pressuring President Roosevelt?

4. What do you think A. Philip Randolph meant when he said, "There are some things Negroes must do alone"?

5. What was the result of Executive Order 8802?

Japanese Internment

BY MARY KATHLEEN FLYNN

January 1, 1942

Dear Diary,

This is a brand-new journal I'm starting on the first day of a brand-new year, 1942! I am 12 years old, and I am in seventh grade. My name is Setsuko. It was my English teacher's idea to keep a journal— she thinks it will help us students write better.

Last night was New Year's Eve, but it didn't feel like New Year's Eve. Nobody in my family wanted to celebrate because the country is at war, and my older brother is a soldier.

This war has been going on a long time in Europe, but now the United States is in it too. It's embarrassing to me why the U.S. is involved in the war. It's because Japan made a surprise attack on

Signs in the window of a Japanese-American–owned store in Los Angeles demonstrate the owners' patriotism.

<u>Pearl Harbor</u> in Hawaii last month. My parents were both born in Japan, and it's strange to think that their homeland is now our enemy.

I live in San Francisco, and there are many Japanese Americans here. I think many of us feel ashamed to be Japanese right now. But we also feel ashamed for feeling ashamed—if that makes sense!

It's nice to be able to confide in my journal!

* * *

February 2, 1942

Dear Diary,

Today was a bad day. Because we're Japanese, my family's life in San Francisco has become very awkward. Suddenly, people look at us funny. I don't understand what they're thinking. I've never even been to Japan! And my older brother is a soldier in the United States Army.

This afternoon when my sisters and I were walking home from school, a group of older boys followed us down the street. They called us spies.

People and Terms to Know

Pearl Harbor—major naval base in Hawaii where the U.S. Pacific fleet was docked when Japan made a surprise attack on December 7, 1941. The attack brought the United States into World War II.

We just put our heads down and kept walking as quickly as we could. We were so scared.

Even when we got to our apartment building, I was afraid the boys were going to follow us inside. But then across the street, Mr. Kelly, who owns the newsstand, yelled at the boys to think about the countries where their own parents came from.

> *We just put our heads down and kept walking as quickly as we could. We were so scared.*

I hope they don't follow us home from school tomorrow!

* * *

February 20, 1942

Dear Diary,

Things are getting worse. Tonight at dinner, my father told us that the president of the United States, Franklin Delano Roosevelt, had signed an important document called **Executive Order 9066**.

People and Terms to Know

Executive Order 9066—President Franklin Roosevelt's order that set up areas in the United States as military zones in which ordinary citizens were not allowed. This law allowed the government to move Japanese Americans out of these areas, which were usually just regular neighborhoods in cities.

Father explained that this executive order means the U.S. Army can declare an area, like our neighborhood in San Francisco, a military area and then kick out anyone it wants!

Father said some Americans want to see us locked up in camps like military bases—he called it **internment**. He says people don't trust us anymore. They think that if Japan invaded San Francisco, we'd work as spies for the Japanese government!

I've never been outside of San Francisco, and I can't imagine living anywhere else. San Francisco is so pretty with all the hills and the beautiful bay and the new Golden Gate Bridge. I even have a view! The bedroom that my sisters and I share has a window that looks down the hill, and I can see a little sliver of the bay. I hope we don't get kicked out! I love our home!

*   *   *

People and Terms to Know

internment—act of forcing people to stay in a certain place, especially during wartime.

April 1, 1942

Dear Diary,

It's April Fool's Day, but nobody in my family is making any jokes because we got bad news today. We have to leave our home very soon. As we feared, our neighborhood has been turned into a military area, and the government says all people of Japanese ancestry have to leave. We have to get out by next Tuesday, April 7—less than a week!

At bedtime, my mother looked around our bedroom and told us girls we would have to start packing soon. She said we needed to decide which clothes and toys we absolutely had to have. She doesn't think we'll be allowed to take many things with us.

What will happen to my dolls and my dollhouse? Even though I'm too old to play with dolls, I don't want to give them up!

*   *   *

April 6, 1942

Dear Diary,

This is the last night I will sleep in my own bed in my own home. Our bedroom looks very bare tonight. We have spent the last week selling or giving away everything that we owned. My mother cried when we sold the furniture, and my father said we got far less money than it was worth. We sold everything we could, even my father's camera, which he loved.

We sold everything we could, even my father's camera, which he loved.

We're each allowed to take two suitcases or duffel bags, but we have to carry them ourselves, so they can't be too heavy. We have to bring our own sheets and blankets, and also a plate, cup, and silverware. I'm bringing some clothes, three of my favorite books, some paper and pencils, and, of course, you, dear Diary.

This afternoon, I gave my dolls and dollhouse to Mr. Kelly's daughter. She's only four years old, and she clapped her hands with delight when I gave them to her. I hope she will take good care of them.

* * *

May 3, 1942

Dear Diary,

We've had a hard time the last few weeks, and I've had no privacy to write anything in my journal.

After we left our home in San Francisco, a Greyhound bus took us to a huge racetrack. There were hundreds of Japanese people and American soldiers, and it was very confusing. We had to stay there several days before a special train took us to our new home, a big camp called **Manzanar**.

Manzanar is very different from San Francisco. For one thing, the ocean is a long way away. And the weather here is weird. It can be hot and windy all day and then freezing cold at night. My sisters and I sleep in our clothes to keep warm.

We are finally starting to settle into our new home. I say home, but really it's just one small room for all five of us. It's as if our whole family were squeezed into the little bedroom my sisters and I shared in San Francisco. We sleep on cots. My parents each have their own cot, but my sisters and I have to double up because our family only has four cots.

I should be grateful, though; as my mother says, at least our family is together—except for my brother who's a soldier in the war.

I know I shouldn't say it, but I don't feel grateful. I can't help seeing how ugly everything is here. The

People and Terms to Know

Manzanar—town in inland California that was empty until it was turned into a relocation center for Japanese Americans in March 1942.

▲

Japanese Americans try to keep their spirits up at the Manzanar, California, internment camp in April 1942.

buildings are all made of wood, and they all look alike. They're covered with tar-paper, which is ugly. My mother said the buildings are called **barracks**.

There's no kitchen in our "home," just a small stove for heat but not for cooking. We eat our meals

---

People and Terms to Know

barracks—building or group of buildings for housing soldiers, workers, or other large numbers of people.

---

in a cafeteria with everyone else, and the food tastes terrible. I miss my mother's cooking. We also have to go to another building to wash up or go to the bathroom. It's very depressing.

*   *   *

May 30, 1942

Dear Diary,

I am starting to get used to living at Manzanar.

Everybody here is trying to make the best of the situation—and to make our lives here as much like the way we used to live as possible.

They have opened up a school here, and my sisters and I go to it every day. The school building looks just like all the other buildings. One nice thing is that some of our friends from our old school are here, too. Our teachers are like regular teachers, although half of them are Japanese Americans like we are. They live here too.

A lot of the grownups are bored and don't know quite what to do with themselves, but some of the men have jobs. My father has a new road construction job. He seems to be much more cheerful since he started working again.

My mother also seems happier than she has in months. She and some of the other women who live in our building have begun to plant a garden. They are trying to make the camp look as pretty—and as much like home—as possible. Of course it's hard to make the camp look like home. There is no ocean here!

My parents say the war won't last forever, and one day we'll go back to San Francisco. As for me, I can't wait to see the ocean again!

QUESTIONS TO CONSIDER

1. Why did the United States get involved in World War II?

2. Why did Setsuko feel both ashamed to be Japanese and ashamed that she was ashamed?

3. Why did some people think Japanese Americans were dangerous?

4. How did Japan's attack on Pearl Harbor change life for Japanese Americans who lived in San Francisco?

5. How would you feel if you and your family had to leave your home and live in an internment camp?

The Children of Topaz: The Story of a Japanese-American Internment Camp Based on a Classroom Diary
By Michael O. Tunnell and George W. Chilcoat

This collection of real diary entries from a third-grade class in a desert relocation camp details students' daily lives and thoughts. The authors also include photographs and commentary.

The Moved-Outers
By Florence Crannell Means

In this novel, Sue, a typical high school student, must move with her Japanese-American family to an internment camp during World War II.

I Am an American: The True Story of Japanese Internment
By Jerry Stanley

Photo-essays and interviews in this book depict the lives and feelings of the people sent to internment camps.

The Zoot Suit Riots

BY MARIANNE McCOMB

Los Angeles, California
June 19, 1943

My Sweetheart,

Lo siento—I'm sorry—that I haven't written in over two weeks, but my darling Pedro, Los Angeles has gone completely mad! Our beloved "City of Angels" is not the place it was when you shipped out overseas. East Los Angeles is a war zone now, and I awaken each morning with fear in my heart.

Pedro, I remember so well the day you enlisted in the army. I was so proud—but I was so scared too! I remember the shock in my Papa's eyes when you told him you were going off to serve your country. When he objected, you told him that you owed a great debt to America, the land of opportunity.

Frank H. Tellez, 22, wears his zoot suit at the Los Angeles County Jail in 1943.

You reminded Papa how you had come here from Mexico when you were just a child, and it had seemed to you that Los Angeles had welcomed you. There were jobs for your parents, schools for your brothers and sisters, and food on the table every night for dinner. "For this, I am grateful," you said, "and I must show my gratitude by serving in the army." And then you left, and I thought my heart would burst with pride and sadness.

But now, Pedro, a year has gone by, and the America you left behind is no longer the America of your dreams. No, it is not, and it hurts me to have to tell you this.

The last time I wrote, I told you about the **evacuation** of the Japanese Americans living on the West Coast. These poor people, whom the government calls a "threat to national security," have all been sent away to **relocation centers** in the desert. They were forced to leave behind their homes, their businesses, and their freedom—all

---

People and Terms to Know

evacuation—movement of people out of a threatened area.

relocation centers—concentration camps located in the western United States during World War II. The Japanese and Japanese-American population on the West Coast was moved to these camps after Japan bombed Pearl Harbor, Hawaii.

because the government decided they were "the enemy." I watched all this happen, Pedro, with my own eyes, and I didn't have the courage to protest. I had none of your bravery, so I stayed silent.

I watched all this happen, Pedro, with my own eyes, and I didn't have the courage to protest.

But since the Japanese left, things have grown worse in Los Angeles. Now those who unjustly picked on Japanese Americans have turned their eyes on our community—our people!—and begun **persecuting** us. There have been reports in the local papers about a "Mexican Crime Wave" and "**Zoot Suit** Criminals." Pedro, these reports would make me laugh if they weren't so frightening. There is no Mexican crime wave! It is a lie! And you yourself have worn your zoot suit with pride, and I know you are no criminal.

Every day, the newspapers print more and more of these lies. Several months ago, the Los Angeles sheriff's department appointed a man named E. Duran Ayres to investigate the "crime wave." His

---

People and Terms to Know

persecuting—causing to suffer repeatedly.
Zoot Suit—man's suit with a long, tight-fitting jacket having wide, padded shoulders and baggy trousers tapering down to tight cuffs. They were popular with Latino men in the early 1940s.

report was an outrage to all of us. He said that Mexican Americans are violent at heart and will never change their ways. Our violent tendencies, he explained, come from our ancestors—the "blood-thirsty" <u>Aztecs</u> of hundreds of years ago.

When I read Ayres's report, my heart beat as fast as a bird's. I felt so scared for the safety of my family. How could people think such things? Was this how everyone in America felt?

But my brother Carlos, he was not scared. He was furious! He cleaned and ironed his zoot suit and put it on, not caring that others might think him a criminal. I told Carlos that it wasn't safe for him to gather with other zoot-suiters on our streets. He refused to listen to me. He said that America is free, and that he will not live in fear of people who are prejudiced. Then he turned away from me and walked out the door.

All this hatred toward our people came to a head a couple of weeks ago. This is what happened, *querido*, dear one. On June 3, eleven sailors who

---

People and Terms to Know

Aztecs—Mexican Indians whose nation was at its height when Spain invaded Mexico in 1519.

U.S. Navy sailors armed with clubs, pipes, and bottles look for zoot-suiters.

were on shore leave in Los Angeles said they were attacked by a group of Mexican thugs. In response, two hundred uniformed sailors took cabs and buses into our community. I heard these men, these men in uniform who had sworn to protect our citizens, screaming horrible things. They were throwing bottles and breaking windows and chasing Latino children back into their houses.

I ran into Papa's room to warn my parents. I found only Mama, who was sobbing. She said that Papa had gone to look for Carlos, who was out on the streets somewhere.

We could not call the police or the sheriff. It seemed that all of Los Angeles was against us.

All night long, Mama and I sat up and waited for Papa and Carlos to return home. We heard reports that the zoot-suiters were being beaten and stripped of their clothes. We were so frightened that we stayed on our knees the whole night, praying for the safety of Papa and Carlos.

The next morning, Papa and Carlos came home. Papa was unhurt, but Carlos had blood dripping down the side of his face. His clothes were torn, and he was bruised all over. Mama and I ran to him and put our arms around him. He started to sob, and so did we. But what could we do, Pedro? We could not call the police or the sheriff. It seemed that all of Los Angeles was against us.

Over the next few days things got worse, not better. More and more uniformed sailors came ashore and charged into the heart of our community.

Soon, soldiers from the army joined them as well, and they marched four-by-four down the streets of East Los Angeles. They broke into homes, offices, bars, and restaurants and attacked any zoot-suiter that dared cross their path. The newspapers called these servicemen "heroes," but they were not! They were criminals, and their victims were men, women, and children of Hispanic descent.

Finally, on June 7, military officials did what the police of Los Angeles refused to do. They moved in to stop the rioting and said that Los Angeles was off-limits for all military personnel. But the military never punished its men, and the police department never arrested a single rioter. Could it be that our community matters so little to the people in charge?

Pedro, I wonder if I've lost all hope for America. How can we marry and raise children in a place that hates us so much? Will I have to live in fear that an **Anglo** will spit in my face or trip my babies as they take their first steps—simply because we are from Mexico? Is that what our lives will be like?

People and Terms to Know

Anglo—informal term for a white American who is not of Hispanic descent.

Please write, Pedro, and tell me that I'm wrong. I so want to be brave like you, but I don't understand this war we're fighting in the streets of Los Angeles. Will it ever end?

Your ever-loving,
Maria

QUESTIONS TO CONSIDER

1. Why did the Zoot Suit Riots take place?

2. What is Maria's attitude toward the riots? How does she feel once they are over?

3. Why do you think Carlos continued to wear his zoot suit even after the zoot-suiters were called criminals in the newspapers?

4. Why do you think the police failed to protect East Los Angeles residents from those in the military who rioted in their neighborhood?

5. How would you feel if you were Pedro, serving in the U.S. Army, and you received this letter from Maria?

6. How do you think someone's appearance, such as wearing a certain kind of clothing, might make someone else angry or violent?

Mama and the Ball Game

BY STEPHEN CURRIE

So it's a lazy summer day, the kind where you gotta do *some*thing, only you don't know what. Hank Jenkins says we oughta go to the movies. But we went yesterday and the picture was *bad*. So that's out.

I say, maybe a bike race. But last time we did that, Hank busted his bike and busted his elbow too. Our folks warned us, if anybody else gets hurt in a bike race, there ain't gonna *be* no more bikes. So that's out too.

Then Willie Gibson pipes up, "Well, how's about the Reds game?"

Me and Hank look at each other. That Willie, he ain't so sharp to look at him, but now and then he

Jackie Robinson at bat.

comes out with something real smart. <u>Crosley Field</u> ain't so far off, and it don't cost much to get in.

I stand up off the front stoop. "Let me tell my—"

The kitchen window upstairs slides open. Mama looks out the window. Her big brown eyes stare down at me, hard. "Where you off to, Louie?"

I wave up to her. "I'm going to the Reds game, Mama. All right?"

"The *Reds?*" Mama frowns. "Who're they playing today?"

Huh? Mama don't know nothin' about baseball. What does she care who the Reds are playing?

"The <u>Dodgers</u>, Miz Banks," Willie calls out.

"The Dodgers?" Mama stares at him hard. "The ones with <u>Jackie Robinson</u>?"

This time Hank does the talking. "That's right, ma'am."

"Hold on." The kitchen window slams shut. Next thing we know, Mama's standing in the doorway, holding her big going-out purse. "Ready, boys?" she says. "I'm coming with you today."

People and Terms to Know

Crosley Field—ballpark in Cincinnati, Ohio, that in 1947 was the home stadium of the Cincinnati Reds.

Dodgers—Brooklyn Dodgers, the New York City team that signed Jackie Robinson.

Jackie Robinson—(1919–1972) first 20th-century African American to play major league baseball.

* * *

Crosley Field is *packed* with fans. I've never seen so many people at a game. Most of the time, it's mainly white folks, but today there's lots of black folks here too. We get seats in right field, and I'm squished. It seems like Mama's purse takes up half the bench.

*Crosley Field is **packed** with fans. I've never seen so many people at a game.*

But we're lucky we got seats. Some people are standing.

I ain't never seen Mama come to a game before. "Hey, Mama," I say. "How come *you're* here?"

She points to the field where the Dodgers are warming up, to the man wearing number 42. "I'm here for *him*," she says.

"Number 42," says Willie; "why, that's Jackie Robinson. I know all *about* him. He's the first black man to play in the major leagues."

"I know all about him too," says Hank. "He used to play in the **Negro leagues**."

People and Terms to Know

Negro leagues—professional baseball leagues in which all the players were African American. The first all-black professional team, the Cuban Giants, organized in 1885. The first league began in 1920. The Negro leagues folded after the 1948 season, when the Brooklyn Dodgers hired Jackie Robinson.

"Yeah," says Willie. "Then **Mr. Rickey** signed him up for the Dodgers."

I give Willie and Hank a look. I know all that about Robinson—more, too. I know he came up from the minor leagues just this year, even though a lot of fans and players didn't think a black man should play in the majors.

I heard that even some of his own teammates didn't want him. I read how other players yelled at him, cursed him, and tried to hurt him with their spikes, and how he just kept on playing.

Okay, I think, it's kind of a big deal, the first of our people to play major league baseball. But it ain't *that* big a deal.

"It's just baseball," I say. "It's just a game."

Mama looks at me kind of sideways, and she shakes her head.

"It ain't just a game today," she tells me.

* * *

People and Terms to Know

Mr. Rickey—Branch Rickey, president of the Brooklyn Dodgers when it became the first major league baseball team to hire an African-American player.

"**N**ow batting for Brooklyn," says the announcer. "Number 42, the first baseman—Jackie Robinson!"

Mama's up on her feet, and she's clapping just as hard as she can clap. She's clapping so hard it must be hurting her hands.

"Stand up, Louie," she whispers to me, so I stand up, and so do Willie and Hank. We clap too, even Willie, and he's a big Reds fan.

There are boos from the crowd too. Some of the fans behind us yell out ugly names. But Mama just keeps clapping. "Listen, honey," says Mama. "Ain't it grand?"

I listen. And suddenly I don't hear the names or the boos. All I hear is applause from all over the ballpark. If you kind of half-close your eyes, it sounds just like a rain storm—maybe like ocean waves. I never heard that kind of sound before at a game. It makes me kind of goose-pimply all over.

At last we stop clapping and sit down. Robinson swings at the first pitch and hits it into the outfield. It's a double. We cheer, we yell, and we clap some more.

I'm still squished.

* * *

N ext time up, Robinson walks, steals second, and scores a run. Mama's palms *gotta* be sore from all the clapping. The Dodgers lead by two runs, but then the Reds score and it's down to one.

▲
Jackie Robinson leaps to catch a ball.

Mama's wilting in the heat. She buys herself a couple of Cokes. But she still looks hot.

In the ninth inning, the Reds come to bat. They get men on second and third with two outs. A hit will give the Reds the game. "Uh-oh," says Willie, who knows the players best. "Frankie Baumholtz is coming up. That man can flat *hit*."

And then from out of nowhere comes Jackie Robinson. He dives with his back to home plate.

I give him a look. "I thought you was a Reds fan," I say.

"I *was*," says Willie. "Not today."

Mama opens up her purse and takes out a cloth. She wipes her face and sets the purse back down.

Baumholtz swings and pops one down the right field line. The right fielder runs over. The second baseman does too. *Uh-oh.* They're gonna be too late.

Mama rises. "Catch it, Jackie!" she bellows.

And then from out of nowhere comes Jackie Robinson. He dives with his back to home plate. He sticks out his mitt—

Thunk!

The ball lands in the glove and *sticks*.

"Yer out!" yells the umpire at Baumholtz. The game's over. The Dodgers win!

Mama yells and cheers and bangs those hands together. I take a quick peek up at her. I've never seen her look so proud, except maybe the day I won the spelling bee at school.

Jackie Robinson gets up. He looks straight at us. Then his face crinkles up into a smile. And he tosses the ball *our way*.

"I got it!" calls Willie. "Mine!" I yell. "No, mine!" hollers Hank.

"No, *mine*," says Mama, and what do you know but that ball lands smack in the middle of her open purse.

* * *

"Say, Mama," I tell her on the way home. "I've been going to Reds games for my whole life, and I've never caught a ball. Don't you wanna give that one to me?"

She smiles. "First," she says, "you gotta learn a little more about history."

"What's history got to do with baseballs?" Hank asks.

"Someday you're gonna understand exactly why I came to the game today," she says. "You'll understand why Jackie Robinson matters, even to people who ain't baseball fans. You'll know why this ball ain't just an ordinary baseball." She touches my forehead and smiles again. "The day you figure that out, Louie, that's the day you get the ball."

Jackie Robinson had quite a season back in '47.

History. Huh. "This is a trick to get me to study harder in school, right?" I say.

Mama laughs. She kisses me. She hugs me tight. "I love you, sweetie," she tells me.

It's nice to be loved, but in front of the guys?

I roll my eyes.

Aw, *Mama.*

*   *   *

Jackie Robinson had quite a season back in '47. All the man did was lead the league in stolen bases, score 125 runs, and win the award given to the best new player in the major leagues that year—oh, and prove that African Americans could play baseball as well as anybody.

Jackie was the first black man in the majors, but he wasn't the only one—not by a long shot. Later that year, Cleveland put Larry Doby in their lineup. A little while after that came Roy Campanella and Monte Irvin, Minnie Minoso and Don Newcombe. Pretty soon the Negro leagues went out of business; all the good players were in the majors.

By the time Jackie called it a career, he'd played in the majors for 10 years. He was one of the great ones. He was an All-Star five times, he won the **Most Valuable Player** trophy once, and he was elected to baseball's Hall of Fame on his first try.

The Reds didn't get their first African-American players till 1954. That's when Willie started cheering for them again. As for me, I don't pay so much attention to baseball these days, but when I do look at the standings I still find myself rooting for the Dodgers. It's funny how that works—all those years, all those players, but somehow it still seems to go back to the man who made it all possible.

Oh, and what happened to the baseball? You remember the one, it landed in Mama's purse at Crosley Field back in '47. She said she'd give it to me when I figured out why it wasn't any ordinary ball.

I've got it in my study.

People and Terms to Know

Most Valuable Player—baseball award given to the player who did the most to help his team.

And believe me, after all these years I know *exactly* why it was no ordinary ball.

QUESTIONS TO CONSIDER

1. What makes Mama come to the baseball game?

2. How did fans react to Robinson when he first came to the major leagues? Why did they react the way they did?

3. What do you think Mama means when she says, "This ball ain't just an ordinary baseball"?

4. How do you feel about the Negro leagues going out of business?

5. What do you think was the hardest part of being the first African-American player in the major leagues? Why?

Jackie Robinson
(Black Americans of Achievement)
By Richard Scott and Nathan I. Huggins

In-depth look at Robinson's life, complete with pictures and a forward by Coretta Scott King.

Jackie and Me: A Baseball Card Adventure
By Dan Gutman and Joe Stoshack

This book is a fictionalized account of a boy who travels back in time to meet his hero, Jackie Robinson.

Jackie's Nine:
Jackie Robinson's Rules to Live By
By Jackie Robinson and Sharon Robinson

Jackie Robinson describes the values and beliefs that helped him succeed against large odds.

The Civil Rights Movement

The Montgomery Bus Boycott

BY DANNY MILLER

Viola Warfield and her granddaughter Patty were baking Christmas cookies. Since she had retired from law, Viola was able to spend a lot more time with her 11-year-old granddaughter.

"Tell me the story about the bus, Grandma," Patty begged, sifting flour into a large ceramic bowl.

"Oh, child," Viola replied, "you've heard that story so many times you could tell it yourself!"

"Not since I was 10, Grandma. I understand things a lot better now!"

It was early December in Montgomery, Alabama. The day was surprisingly cold for that part of the country. Her granddaughter's request made Viola remember another cold December day, so many years ago. Viola stopped beating the eggs into the batter and thought back to how it all began.

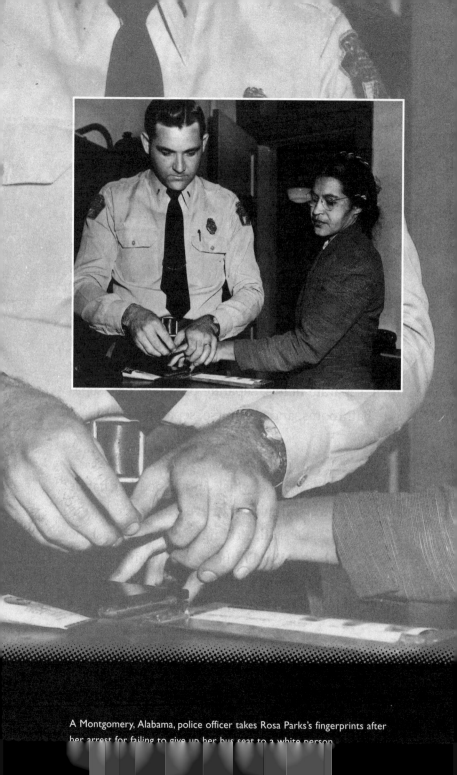

A Montgomery, Alabama, police officer takes Rosa Parks's fingerprints after her arrest for failing to give up her bus seat to a white person.

"It was December 1, 1955," Viola said. "I was just 18 years old, and I was on my way home after working at the drug store.

"I was on the Cleveland Avenue bus, sitting in what they called the 'colored section' at the back of the bus."

"I can't believe you couldn't sit wherever you wanted to, Grandma," Patty said. "That was so unfair!"

"Oh, that was just one of the **segregation** laws we had to live with in those days, child. They had separate restaurants for blacks and whites back then, separate hotels, separate park benches, separate bathrooms, and, of course, separate schools."

Viola set down the whisk and wiped her hands on her apron. "I think out of everything we had to deal with," she said, "riding the buses was the worst. We had to get on the bus through the front door, drop our dime into the fare box, get off the bus, and then get on again through the rear door.

People and Terms to Know

segregation—policy and practice of separating different groups such as races of people, particularly to discriminate against people of color in a white society.

"Once we were on the bus, we could only sit in the back. If a white person got on and there were no more seats in the front of the bus, the driver made us give up our seats so that the white person could sit down. I knew some people, black and white, who wouldn't even ride the bus because they thought these laws were so awful. But most of us didn't have a choice. My family didn't own a car back then, so I had to ride the bus to and from work every day."

> *"If a white person got on and there were no more seats in the front of the bus, the driver made us give up our seats."*

"So what happened when <u>**Rosa Parks**</u> got on the bus, Grandma?" Patty asked.

"Mrs. Parks got on at the stop after me and found a seat in the first row of the 'colored section.' In those days Rosa did sewing over at the Montgomery Fair department store. I could see she was tired after a long day of work."

"Did you know her well, Grandma?" Patty asked. She had heard this story before, but it seemed to get better with each telling.

People and Terms to Know

Rosa Parks—(b. 1913) African American whose refusal to give up her seat on a bus in Montgomery, Alabama, in 1955 led to a Supreme Court decision outlawing bus segregation.

"We always said hello to each other, but that's about all. My cousin Alberta lived in the same housing complex as Rosa and her husband Raymond. We knew that Mrs. Parks was a fine woman who worked for our local branch of the NAACP.

"A lot more people got on at the next stop. One white man didn't have a seat. The driver called out for the people in the first row of the 'colored section' to give up their seats so that the white man could sit down. They all had to move because it was against the law for a black person to sit in the same row as a white person!"

"Oh, Grandma," Patty said, "how could our own city have had such terrible rules?"

"Honey, I'm glad you live in a world where such things are hard to understand!"

"So, did everyone in that row get up?" Patty asked.

"Everyone but Mrs. Parks. I was sitting with my friend Gina Peoples and we looked at each other right away. We just knew something big was about to happen.

"Sure enough, the driver stopped the bus and went over to Mrs. Parks. 'I told you I wanted the seat,' he said. 'Are you going to stand up?' Mrs. Parks just sat there, as calm as could be and said

'No, I'm not.' Three simple words, Patty, but it seemed like our lives were never the same again!

"Well, you can imagine how this got the bus driver going. Before we knew it, he had pulled the bus over, and two police officers came on board and arrested Rosa right there on the spot! Until my dying day, I'll never forget the sight of those officers taking Mrs. Parks off that bus and into their patrol car to drive her to jail."

Viola was now beating the flour Patty had sifted into the batter with a large wooden spoon. The more she talked about Rosa Parks's arrest, the harder she beat the batter.

"Gina and I couldn't wait to get home and tell everyone what had happened. You never saw word spread so fast. Within a few hours it seemed like every black person in Montgomery knew the full story.

"Somebody called up **E. D. Nixon**, the head of the Montgomery NAACP, and he got Rosa out of jail. Her trial was set for Monday, and Nixon got

People and Terms to Know

E. D. Nixon—(1899–1987) African-American leader, president of the Montgomery NAACP during the early days of the Civil Rights movement.

Fred Gray, one of Montgomery's few African-American lawyers, to represent her.

"A group of us decided to meet that night at the Dexter Avenue Baptist Church. The new pastor there was a young man named **Martin Luther King, Jr.**"

> *"A group of us decided to meet that night at the Dexter Avenue Baptist Church. The new pastor there was a young man named Martin Luther King, Jr."*

"That's so great that you got to meet Dr. King," Patty said.

"It was, honey, but remember that he wasn't well known in those days. He had just moved to Montgomery the year before, and his wife Coretta had just had a baby girl.

"Some people thought Rosa's trial was the perfect place to challenge some of the segregation laws we'd all had to deal with for so long, especially on the buses.

"E. D. Nixon said that on the day of Rosa's trial we should all **boycott** the buses. We printed up

---

People and Terms to Know

Martin Luther King, Jr.—(1929–1968) Baptist minister and civil rights leader who encouraged the use of non-violent methods. Awarded the Nobel Peace Prize in 1964, he was assassinated in 1968.

boycott—stop using something for a period of time as an act of protest.

▲

Martin Luther King, Jr. preaches to supporters in Montgomery. King organized the bus boycott that protested Parks's arrest.

leaflets and called everyone we knew. And that Sunday, every black minister in town told the folks in his church to join the boycott."

"But, Grandma," Patty asked, "how did everyone get to work that day?"

"Lots of people walked. We organized carpools. We got the African-American taxicab companies to pitch in. Everyone in the community worked together!

"When Gina and I walked to work that morning, the 5 miles seemed like 5 blocks! We were joined by more and more people along the way—it felt like a big party for freedom. And whenever we saw a big empty bus go by, we cheered and hollered!

"Mrs. Parks was found guilty, of course. She was fined and released, but her lawyer said he'd **appeal** the case." Viola started greasing the cookie sheets with a dab of butter she held with wax paper.

"That night, so many people showed up at the church they had to set up speakers outside so that everyone could hear Martin Luther King speak. Patty, you never heard a man speak like Pastor King!"

Viola closed her eyes and strained to remember King's exact words:

"'We are here because we are American citizens, and we are determined to apply our citizenship to the fullest of its means. . . . There comes a time when people get tired of being trampled by the iron feet of oppression.' That night, we decided to continue the bus boycott until we got some kind of justice."

"Did it work, Grandma?" Patty asked, dropping tablespoonfuls of batter onto the cookie sheets.

"Oh, it was hard. Lots of us were arrested, houses were bombed, people beaten up, cars stopped for speeding when they weren't going faster than a crawl. Hate groups like the **Ku Klux Klan** tried to scare us every day. But we stood together and continued on. It was that boycott that made me want to become a lawyer and work on **civil rights** cases.

> *"Lots of us were arrested, houses were bombed, people beaten up, cars stopped for speeding when they weren't going faster than a crawl."*

"Finally, on December 20, 1956—just a little more than a year after the boycott began, the U.S. Supreme Court ruled that the segregation laws on the Montgomery buses were **unconstitutional**. The case gave hope to African-American people all over the country, who started changing things in their own cities and towns."

Viola now removed the trays from the oven and used a spatula to lift the golden sugar cookies onto a plate. The cookies smelled so delicious that Patty

---

People and Terms to Know

Ku Klux Klan—secret organization violently opposed to African Americans, Jews, Catholics, and foreigners. It uses terrorist methods, such as bombings and setting fires, as well as legal methods such as marches, to spread its hatred.

civil rights—rights belonging to a person as a citizen of a free society.

unconstitutional—not in agreement with the U.S. Constitution; illegal.

couldn't wait for them to cool. She grabbed one right away.

"So you see, honey," Viola said, enjoying a bite of a cookie herself, "that one small action of Mrs. Parks set into motion a movement that changed the lives of millions of people!"

"Now, that's what I call a hero," Patty said.

QUESTIONS TO CONSIDER

1. Why did African-American people in Montgomery have to sit in the back of the bus in the 1950s?

2. How would you feel if you had to sit on separate park benches, use separate bathrooms, or go to a separate school because of the color of your skin?

3. Why do you think Rosa Parks refused to give up her seat that day in 1955?

4. How did people in Montgomery learn about Mrs. Parks's arrest and the bus boycott?

5. How did the African-American community in Montgomery work together during the yearlong boycott?

6. What do you think Martin Luther King, Jr., meant when he spoke of "the iron feet of oppression"?

7. How did the bus boycott finally end?

The Little Rock Nine Enter Central High

BY JUDITH CONAWAY

Have you got that tape recorder working? Here we go. I'm remembering my senior year at Central High School, in Little Rock, Arkansas. That was the 1957–1958 school year, the first year of **integration**. I'll just go down this list of your questions, if you all don't mind.

First question: "Did you know that your school was going to be in the history books?"

Well, certainly our parents and teachers tried to make us see it. They'd say things like, "The whole world is going to be watching how you

---

People and Terms to Know

integration—putting groups together that had been apart; racial integration means making public facilities, such as schools and parks, open to people of all races.

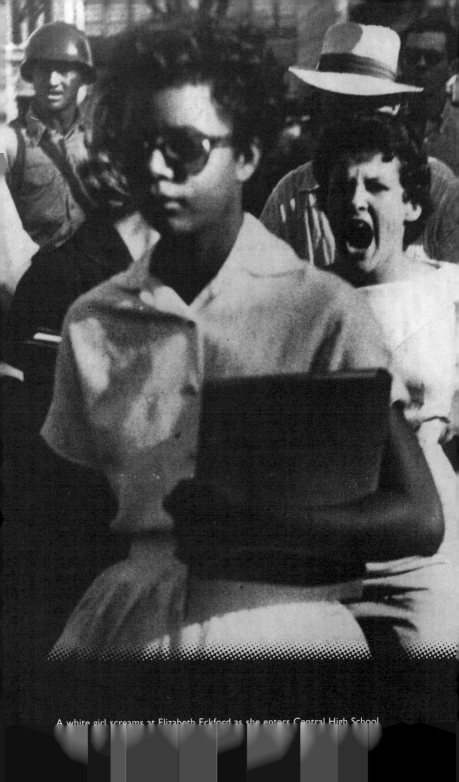
A white girl screams at Elizabeth Eckford as she enters Central High School.

behave," or "People are going to judge Little Rock by your behavior."

So they told us we were making history, but it didn't sink in. My friends and I were all pretty self-centered back then, as I recall. Of course, people tend to be at that age. I don't remember thinking too deeply about anything, really. I was too busy daydreaming about **Elvis**, probably.

Next question: "What do you remember about attitudes toward race in Little Rock in 1957?"

Well, that question's the big one, isn't it? As a society, we've buried a lot of the old racist attitudes. But they're still there sometimes, hidden. So I'm going to be careful what I say here.

What I remember is that white people and black people saw each other all the time, and lived near each other, but didn't mix socially. We were led to believe that both sides preferred it that way.

My sisters and I were raised to treat colored people with respect. That's what "nice" people did. "Nice" was a very big concept with my mama. We

---

People and Terms to Know

Elvis—Elvis Presley (1935–1977), most famous of the early rock and roll singers. By 1957, Elvis had recorded hits such as "Heartbreak Hotel," "Hound Dog," and "Don't Be Cruel."

had a Negro housekeeper, Mrs. Green, and "nice" was very big with her too. "Nice" behavior did not include dirty words or name-calling of any kind. As for other racial attitudes—well, I'd prefer not to dwell on them any more. I'd rather go on to the next question.

They said people who joined civil rights groups were "troublemakers."

"What do you remember about the beginning of school in 1957?"

I can remember the tension building up. A neighbor took Mama aside and repeated a rumor that Mrs. Green had joined the National Association for the Advancement of Colored People. Some people were firing their help for that, you see. They said people who joined civil rights groups were "troublemakers." But my mother just looked down her nose at the neighbor and said, "In my house, it is not polite to discuss politics."

But even nice people couldn't avoid politics that summer. Remember, this was three whole years after **_Brown_ v. _Board of Education of Topeka_**. After

People and Terms to Know

Brown v. _Board of Education of Topeka_—1954 ruling by the U.S. Supreme Court that said that segregation in the public schools was against the United States Constitution.

that ruling, the Little Rock School Board "bought time" with a six-year gradual integration plan. It was supposed to start in September 1957, with just the high school.

The NAACP took the School Board to court to try and speed up integration. But the judge ruled in favor of the gradual plan. During the summer of 1957, some white groups also went to court, to keep black students out of their schools. But the court ruled that the gradual plan had to go ahead.

Then the **Civil Rights Act of 1957** became law on August 29, right before school started. There was talk that both white and black groups might demonstrate at the school.

On September 2, the day before school started, **Governor Faubus** called out the Arkansas National Guard. They surrounded the whole school. The governor said he was trying to prevent violence, but of course, he was against integration too.

People and Terms to Know

Civil Rights Act of 1957—federal law that established the voting rights of African Americans and punished voting areas that violated these rights.

Governor Faubus—Orval Faubus (1910–1994) governor of Arkansas during the Little Rock Central High integration crisis.

That much became clear on September 4, the second day of classes. That's when the **Little Rock Nine** showed up. On the orders of the governor, the National Guard turned these nine black students away.

But soon a federal judge ordered the governor to remove the National Guard. The Little Rock

White students protest the integration of Little Rock schools.

police moved in to guard the school. They couldn't keep order. By this time there were people rioting in front of the school, making it impossible for the black students to enroll. President Dwight D. Eisenhower finally had to call in the United States Army. The Little Rock Nine entered school under army protection, on September 25, 1957.

It was strange for the first few days, seeing the soldiers in the halls. But then we just got used to them.

That was the first day I actually saw the black students. I remember being surprised that the girls' clothes were just as nice as mine. I also remember being ashamed of the horrible things some of the white students were saying.

The next question on your list is, "What was it like to go to your school under army guard?"

It was strange for the first few days, seeing the soldiers in the halls. But then we just got used to them. All they did was stand around. We girls flirted with the soldiers quite a bit. Most of them were only a little bit older than we were, after all.

Next question: "Did you meet any of the Little Rock Nine in person?"

I'm afraid I didn't, not really. They were in some of my classes. I remember Elizabeth Eckford, the tall girl. She always walked and held herself so proudly. I spoke to her politely a few times, that's all.

I did sometimes sit near the black girls in the cafeteria. One day at lunch some white boys were making fun of them. It was just the usual boy stuff at first. In those days, nice girls were supposed to ignore boys' comments. So we all sat there like little ladies. Then the remarks got ugly and racist.

Finally one of the black girls—Minnijean Brown was her name—just couldn't take it any more. She got up and emptied her bowl of chili all over the guys who were teasing her.

Minnijean Brown got suspended from school because of that incident. A lot of us girls thought it was unfair, because the boys had really gone out of bounds. They were "purely rude and crude," as my mother used to put it.

I wish I could report that after that the black and white girls got along and everything was peachy. They didn't, and it was not. As I recall, the Little Rock Nine stayed in a group by themselves, not really part of the school. That brings me to your last question, "What would you do differently if you could repeat that year?"

Believe me, if it were a movie, I wish I could rewrite that script and reshoot those pictures. I like to imagine myself stepping out of the crowd and giving Elizabeth Eckford a friendly welcome. I fantasize about standing up for Minnijean Brown and helping to call attention to the garbage all of us girls had to put up with from the boys. In my fantasies, I'm one of the heroes.

> *I was the opposite of a hero. I was one of the nice people who did nothing.*

But you can't rewrite history. You can only learn from it. I was the opposite of a hero. I was one of the nice people who did nothing.

The heroes were the Little Rock Nine. They were the scared, lonely teenagers who gave up their own normal high school life to become pioneers for civil rights. They 100 percent deserve the Gold Medals they got from Congress in 1999.

I wish I had been good enough and brave enough to know them better.

QUESTIONS TO CONSIDER

1. What is your opinion of Governor Faubus's actions?

2. What happened when the Little Rock Nine first tried to attend Central High?

3. How did white students at Central High treat the Little Rock Nine?

4. What qualities made the Little Rock Nine heroes?

5. What does the narrator mean when she says, "Believe me, if it were a movie, I wish I could rewrite that script and reshoot those pictures"?

6. If you had been one of the Little Rock Nine, what would have been the hardest part of your high school experience?

On September 24, 1957, President Dwight D. Eisenhower ordered federal troops to Little Rock Central High School. In an address to the American people that same evening, he explained the reasons for his action.

"A foundation of our American way of life is our national respect for law. In the South, as elsewhere, citizens are keenly aware of the tremendous disservice that has been done to the people of Arkansas in the eyes of the nation, and that has been done to the nation in the eyes of the world.

"At a time when we face grave situations abroad because of the hatred that Communism bears toward a system of government based on human rights, it would be difficult to exaggerate the harm that is being done to the prestige and influence, and indeed to the safety, of our nation and the world. Our enemies are gloating over this incident and using it everywhere to misrepresent our whole nation. We are portrayed as a violator of those standards of conduct which the peoples of the world united to proclaim in the Charter of the United Nations. There they affirmed 'faith in fundamental human rights' and 'in the dignity and worth of the human person' and they did so 'without distinction as to race, sex, language, or religion.'

"And so, with deep confidence, I call upon the citizens of the state of Arkansas to assist in bringing to an immediate end all interference with the law and its processes. If resistance to the federal court orders ceases at once, the further presence of federal troops will be unnecessary, and the city of Little Rock will return to its normal habits of peace and order, and a blot upon the fair name and high honor of our nation in the world will be removed.

"Thus will be restored the image of America and of all of its parts as one nation, indivisible, with liberty and justice for all."

"I Have A Dream"

BY BRIAN J. MAHONEY

Why do I always get the *worst* assignments in the **National Park Service**? Where does it say, "Give it to Bob Flanigan"?

I've been hearing about how cops down south have been beating up these protest marchers. Great—now I'm stationed in front of an army of them! Every time these black people look my way, they might see me as some kind of enemy. It's not that I blame them; I just wish I could avoid the whole thing. I wish this was a normal day here in the heart of Washington, D.C., and the most I had to do was direct tourists to the nearest museum.

People and Terms to Know

National Park Service—U.S. agency within the Interior Department responsible for taking care of all federal park land, including the green areas in downtown Washington, D.C., that surround famous monuments and museums.

Martin Luther King Jr. delivers his famous speech at the March on Washington.

Everybody knows I've been on this beat for years, so why can't I get stationed in the back where crowd control is easier? Now we've got the military guarding federal buildings in case there's a riot. And if there is a riot, who are they gonna get first? That's right. The man in uniform, National Park Service Officer Bob Flanigan, that's who.

This is some crowd—I've never seen so many black people in one place! A lot of white people are here too. I hope they all realize that I'm just here to protect the park, the protesters, and the "big guy" when he gets up to speak in front of the Lincoln Memorial! There are lots of senators and other important people here to keep an eye on, too. I'd better stay on my toes. Anyway, all I know is that as soon as Dr. Martin Luther King, Jr., gets up and does his thing, I can go home and eat the wife's chicken pot pie.

I heard King called the march on Washington to force lawmakers to pass the **Civil Rights Act** President Kennedy has been asking for. The bill's supposed to protect the rights of people against discrimination. I'm still not sure what all the

People and Terms to Know

Civil Rights Act—1964 law that gave African Americans the right to use the same schools and public places as anyone else. It made discrimination against anyone by race, color, sex, religion or national origin illegal.

protesting is about—didn't Lincoln make us all equal when he freed the slaves a long time ago?

Wait a second. That big black lady in the polka-dot dress has been eyeing me ever since I got here. She seems harmless, but she's making me nervous—it's creepy, like she knows me or something. It's like she's a schoolteacher wondering why I'm not paying attention. Did I have a black teacher in grade school? No, I'd remember that.

She seems harmless, but she's making me nervous—it's creepy, like she knows me or something. It's like she's a schoolteacher wondering why I'm not paying attention.

Okay, someone's stepping up to speak. It's King. Good, now stay alert, Bob, keep your eyes open and your mouth shut. Hold it—why's that polka-dot lady coming over here?

"Hello, Officer, my name is Brenda Johnson, and I'm from the local National Association for the Advancement of Colored People."

"Nice to meet you, Ma'am. I'm Officer Flanigan. I noticed you watching me. Do we know each other?"

"More than you might think," she says with a sneaky smile. "Anyway, I know that the Park Service counts the people in attendance. Do you know how many people are here today?"

"I heard possibly a quarter million."

Just then, King starts speaking. "Five score years ago a great American, in whose symbolic shadow we stand, signed the **Emancipation Proclamation**. . . . It came as a joyous daybreak to end the long night of captivity. But one hundred years later, we must face the tragic fact that the Negro is still not free. . . ."

That's what I thought—the Emancipation Proclamation set the slaves free, but why does he say that black people are "still not free"? No, Bob, don't listen—watch the crowd.

The polka-dot lady is speaking in my ear. "Officer Flanigan, you look like a nice man. I'm glad to see you listening to someone who knows what he's talking about."

"Ms. Johnson, I'm here to do my job. I'm not supposed to listen."

People and Terms to Know

Emancipation Proclamation—executive order of President Abraham Lincoln that freed the slaves in all regions fighting against the Union.

"Sometimes bending the rules is the only way to make life better," she says like it's a big secret. "That's what Dr. King is talking about. Why don't you just bend the rules a little bit and listen just this once?"

"Okay, Ma'am." I say it more to keep her from bothering me than anything else. But I guess I am kind of listening anyway. I've got to watch that.

King goes on, and I try not to listen. I'm supposed to protect the people who are listening. So I go about scanning the crowd like I always do. I look at my watch a few times and think about dinner in my favorite chair in front of the TV. I can tell King is a great speaker—the entire crowd is hanging on his every word. I'm leaning over to see if anyone got into the reflecting pool when Ms. Johnson taps on my shoulder and brings me up to date.

"Did you hear that, Officer Flanigan? Dr. King just said that the Constitution and Declaration of Independence guarantee all American citizens the same equal rights. But he said that for colored citizens, that promise is just like a bad check that we've come to Washington, D.C., to cash! Ha! But Dr. King still believes that 'bank of justice' will one day give us the equality we deserve. He's got some way with words, doesn't he?"

"Yes, Ma'am."

I try to make myself seem bored, but I'm not. I can't help it. America's promise of equality is like a bad check the government won't cash? King's got a lot of nerve saying that to all these government officials. But I guess he isn't telling the protesters to hate the government, he's asking them to have faith that the government

> *I try to make myself seem bored, but I'm not. I can't help it.*

will see its mistake. Hmm, that's an interesting way to look at it. The polka-dot lady just shakes her head sideways and winks at me.

I start to listen a bit. ". . . 1963 is not an end, but a beginning. Those who hope that the Negro needed to blow off steam and will now be content will have a rude awakening if the nation returns to business as usual."

This man is *warning* the entire nation! Things are going to change whether the government likes it or not. I have to ask the polka dot lady to explain exactly what he means.

"Well, it's been 'business as usual' for the national government to ignore local governments denying us black folk our rights. He's saying that I should be free to use a public restroom when my family buys gas from a white-owned gas station. He's saying that we intend to go to jail instead of giving up our bus seats to white passengers. We should share schools with white folk. He's saying that we are *not* second class citizens."

As she speaks, my eyes rest on a proud-looking black man wearing a big sign that says "I AM A HUMAN BEING." When he looks back at me, I nod and smile as if to say, "It's okay, I think I get it." He nods too. The polka-dot lady notices this silent exchange, and now she's patting me on the back.

King's voice continues to boom across the reflecting pool. "Let us not seek to satisfy our thirst for freedom by drinking from the cup of bitterness and hatred."

A lot of people in the crowd seem to respond to this idea. I feel kind of foolish for being so nervous before. These people are not here to start any riot. King is telling his supporters that they should not have a "distrust of all white people." I suppose that means I've got to start trusting black people a little more too.

The huge crowd listening to Dr. King stretches from the steps of the Lincoln Memorial, past the reflecting pool, to the Washington Monument (at the top of the photograph). August 28, 1963.

". . . for many of our white brothers, as evidenced by their presence here today, have come to realize that their destiny is tied up with our destiny and their freedom is inextricably bound to our freedom. We cannot walk alone. . . ."

So he's not asking for revenge, he's asking for understanding and justice. That's different. He's not saying it's "us against them;" he's saying it's "right against wrong." This isn't the boring stuff I usually hear around here. Wait until I tell the wife about this!

"I get it, Brenda," I say, offering to shake her hand like I want to thank her for something.

She takes my hand and doesn't give it back.

King's words keep pulling at me, at all of us: "I have a dream that one day this nation will rise up and live out the true meaning of its creed: 'We hold these truths to be self evident, that all men are created equal.' I have a dream that one day on the red hills of Georgia the sons of former slaves and the sons of former slave owners will be able to sit down together at the table of brotherhood. . . . I have a dream that my four little children will one day live in a nation where they will not be judged by the color of their skin but by the content of their character. I have a dream today."

We all feel the electricity building in the crowd. Brenda's hand tightens on mine, but I don't care if anyone sees that or not. I squeeze back just as hard as I watch King getting stronger and stronger.

"From every mountainside, let freedom ring. When we let freedom ring, we let it ring from every village and every

We all feel the electricity building in the crowd.

hamlet, from every state and every city, we will be able to speed up that day when all of God's children, black men and white men, Jews and **gentiles**, Protestants and Catholics, will be able to join hands and sing in the words of the old Negro **spiritual**, 'Free at last! Free at last! Thank God Almighty, we are free at last!'"

The man turns away, and the crowd explodes. I lose my hat hugging Brenda Johnson. I guess in some way, King's dream has changed us all.

People and Terms to Know

gentiles—people who do not practice the Jewish faith.
spiritual—African-American religious folk song.

QUESTIONS TO CONSIDER

1. Why did King call for a march on Washington?

2. How did the government respond?

3. How did King use Lincoln and the Emancipation Proclamation to make a point?

4. What was the "business as usual" that King warned against?

5. What do you think King meant when he said about white people that their "destiny is tied up with our destiny and their freedom is inextricably bound to our freedom"?

Malcolm X and Black Power

BY JUDITH LLOYD YERO

Malcolm Little, a man who recently renamed himself el-Hajj Malik el-Shabazz, is dead. But the man we buried today was best known throughout the county, and the world, as **Malcolm X**. He changed his name as thoroughly as he changed the person he was.

He came into the world as Malcolm Little in Omaha, Nebraska. As a young boy, he saw his home in Lansing, Michigan, burned down by a white racist group called the Ku Klux Klan. Two years later, his preacher father was killed. When he was 14, his mother was placed in a mental institution.

People and Terms to Know

Malcolm X—(1925–1965) born Malcolm Little, African-American civil rights leader who advised blacks to organize themselves for political power and take control of their fate. He was assassinated in February 1965.

Influential civil rights leader Malcolm X

When this "country boy" went to Boston, and later New York, he saw that blacks lived a completely different life. It was a world of city temptations, for both black and white people. Of course, many blacks handled these temptations as well as anyone—but not Malcolm. For the next four years, he entered the world of alcohol, drugs, and every kind of hustle you could imagine.

This is how he described it: "I believed that a man should do anything that he was slick enough, or bad and bold enough. . . . Every word I spoke was hip or profane. I would bet that my working vocabulary wasn't two hundred words. I lived and thought like a predatory animal."

For four years, Malcolm was lucky. He wasn't caught or killed. When he was 20, his luck ran out—or perhaps his luck began. He was arrested and sent to prison for stealing. While there, Malcolm's family members wrote to tell him that they had joined a religion called the **Nation of Islam**. They said that

People and Terms to Know

Nation of Islam—Islamic cultural organization, also called the American Muslim Mission or Black Muslim Movement. It originally preached the superiority of the black race and called for a separate black nation. Members are held to high moral standards.

if he gave up cigarettes and stopped eating pork, they could get him out of prison. Malcolm figured they'd come up with some scam, so he went along with it.

"You don't even know your true family name; you wouldn't recognize your true language if you heard it."

When his brother Reginald visited Malcolm in prison, he told Malcolm that the devil's time on earth was up. And that the devil was the white man. After Reginald left, Malcolm began to think about the white people he'd known—like the white men who had burned down his home. There were also the white teachers who told him the best he could hope for was to be a carpenter rather than the lawyer he wanted to be.

Reginald had said, "You don't even know who you are. You don't even know—the white devil has hidden it from you—that you are from a race of people of ancient civilizations and riches in gold and kings. You don't even know your true family name; you wouldn't recognize your true language if you heard it."

Reginald's words left Malcolm with some of the first serious thoughts he'd ever had in his life. His family continued to put pressure on Malcolm to join the Nation of Islam and follow the words of

Elijah Muhammad, a man they called the Messenger of **Allah**.

Malcolm began studying—reading every book he could lay his hands on. He read that the black man had been "brainwashed for hundreds of years." Malcolm grew to believe that the white man had stolen the black man's history.

When he was released from prison, Malcolm went to the Nation of Islam headquarters in Chicago. There he was fascinated by the teachings of Elijah Muhammad. Malcolm felt that these teachings slashed through old beliefs and tried to free the black man's mind from the white man. Malcolm changed his last name to "X"—a custom of Nation of Islam followers. They did this because their family names had been given to them by white slaveholders. Elijah Muhammad was Malcolm's hero, the closest thing to God on earth.

Malcolm X had less and less in common with Malcolm Little. Malcolm X was moral, hardworking,

---

People and Terms to Know

Elijah Muhammad—(1897–1975) leader of the black separatist religious movement known as the Nation of Islam (Black Muslims) during the height of the Civil Rights Era.

Allah—name Muslims give to God.

and driven. And he was a powerful speaker. Soon he was put in charge of a **mosque** in New York, and there developed a large following. Over the next ten years, he became the most effective spokesperson for the Nation of Islam.

Malcolm did not call for integration—blacks and whites sharing resources and doing things together—as did many other civil rights leaders. He called for separation instead. He believed that black people needed to form their own nation in order to get back the culture that had been stolen from them. They needed to break their ties with the white man.

In Malcolm X, black people sensed a man with a mission. He had come from their own—the poorest of the poor. But he had raised himself beyond drugs, alcohol, tobacco, and crime. He was proof that black people could do this for themselves. Malcolm told them about their history and urged them to have self-respect and be self-reliant. Malcolm never looked for any fame for himself. Every time he spoke, he made it clear that Elijah Muhammad was the one who was the Messenger of Allah.

People and Terms to Know

mosque—Muslim place of worship.

Malcolm X is interviewed by reporters.

However, two things began to shake Malcolm's beliefs. By 1964, he had met more and more white men during his travels. He recognized that not all white men were the devils that Elijah insisted they were. Elijah had also committed acts for which any other Muslim would be punished. Malcolm was troubled by Elijah's willingness to lie about his misdeeds rather than admit them.

Malcolm set out on a pilgrimage to <u>Mecca</u>, the holy city of Islam. He watched the way Muslim people of different colors associated with one another. He realized that the hatred against whites that Elijah Muhammad had preached was not the spirit of true Islam. "In the Muslim world . . . I saw all *races*, all *colors*—blue-eyed blonds to black-skinned Africans—in *true* brotherhood! In unity! Living as one! Worshipping as one!"

He realized that the hatred against whites that Elijah Muhammad had preached was not the spirit of true Islam.

Malcolm also traveled to Africa to recapture the spirit of the people from whom the American blacks had come. At the same time, he brought hope to the blacks who continued to fight for their freedom in Africa.

Once again, Malcolm changed his name—this time to el-Hajj Malik el-Shabazz. It was a sign of his

People and Terms to Know

Mecca—city in Saudi Arabia that was the birthplace of Muhammad, the founder of Islam. Muslims believe they should make a trip to Mecca at least once in their lifetime, if they can.

commitment to true Islam. He wrote a friend, "I've had enough of someone else's **propaganda**. I'm for truth, no matter who tells it. I'm for justice, no matter who it is for or against. I'm a human being first and foremost, and as such I'm for whoever and whatever benefits humanity *as a whole.*"

It was only a matter of time before someone tried to silence him.

Malcolm was still trying to come to terms with these new ideas—with the role that he had to play in raising the awareness of blacks. He continued to speak, but two days ago, February 21, 1965, he was gunned down and killed by members of the Black Muslims for whom he had worked so hard.

Malcolm had expected such an end: he had said many negative things about Elijah Muhammad, who was practically worshipped by his followers. It was only a matter of time before someone tried to silence him. But fear for himself didn't stop him from doing the work in which he believed.

People and Terms to Know

propaganda—effort to convince people to support a particular opinion; the term is often used as an insult, to refer to a collection of half-truths or lies.

"I know that societies often have killed the people who have helped to change those societies. And if I can die having brought any light, having exposed any meaningful truth that will help to destroy the racist cancer that is malignant in the body of America—then all of the credit is due to Allah. Only the mistakes have been mine."

QUESTIONS TO CONSIDER

1. Why do you think Malcolm believed what his brother told him about white people?

2. Why did Malcolm Little change his name to Malcolm X?

3. What do you think the religion of Islam taught Malcolm about racial harmony?

4. Why did Malcolm split with the Nation of Islam?

5. Why do you think Malcolm X is important in history?

The Civil Rights Movement Goes North

BY STEPHEN FEINSTEIN

"Go home! We hate blacks!" shouted the angry crowd. It was August 5, 1966, a hot summer day in Chicago's Marquette Park. Ronald Talbot, a young black civil rights activist from Alabama, stood with Martin Luther King, Jr., in the open field. They waited while the civil rights marchers assembled.

Not far from them stood a crowd of about a thousand angry whites. They shouted more hateful words, while waving racist flags and banners. Suddenly someone yelled, "Kill them!" He threw a brick at Ronald, setting off a hail of bricks, rocks, and bottles. Ronald ducked and threw his arms over his head. A brick struck Dr. King just above his

King stands on the balcony of his apartment in the slums of West Chicago.

right ear. The man who believed with all his heart in **nonviolence** stumbled and fell to the ground.

Ronald had a sudden sick feeling in the pit of his stomach. But Dr. King seemed to be okay. He picked himself up, wiping off the blood with a handkerchief. "Maybe we should call off the march," said Ronald. But Dr. King was determined to lead a peaceful march against **discrimination** in housing.

For the past few years, Ronald had been active in the **Civil Rights movement** in the South. He had worked with the **Freedom Riders** to **desegregate** schools and other public places. He had helped to register black voters in Mississippi. He had been part of a huge demonstration against segregation in Birmingham, Alabama, in April 1963. Ronald sang "We Shall Overcome" with Dr. King and thousands of other marchers. Police attacked them with clubs, police dogs, and powerful fire hoses. Many marchers were injured, and Ronald, Dr.

People and Terms to Know

nonviolence—philosophy, policy, or practice of rejecting violence in favor of peaceful actions as a way of reaching a goal.

discrimination—treatment of people based on their belonging to a group, such as a racial group, rather than on their own merit; prejudice.

Civil Rights movement—effort begun in the 1950s to make sure that all U.S. citizens receive the rights guaranteed by the Constitution.

Freedom Riders—people who rode buses throughout the South in the early 1960s to protest segregation of public facilities.

desegregate—get rid of the system of segregation, in which people of different races were kept separate.

King, and about 2,500 others were arrested. But it had all been worth it. The nonviolent protests had led to the passage of important laws such the **Voting Rights Act of 1965**.

Now Ronald wondered whether they would actually achieve anything in Chicago. After all, this was not the South. Would Dr. King's protests be effective in one of the biggest cities in the North? When Dr. King had announced his plan of a demonstration in Chicago, Ronald was puzzled. "Why Chicago?" he asked. Dr. King explained that in spite of everything that had been accomplished in the South, life had not become any better for African Americans living in **ghettos** in America's Northern cities.

Southern blacks could now eat in desegregated restaurants, attend desegregated schools, and vote. Northern blacks already had the vote. Now the time had come to improve living conditions for African Americans who felt trapped in the ghettos. It was time to put an end to their hopelessness and despair.

People and Terms to Know

Voting Rights Act of 1965—federal law that protected the rights of African Americans to vote.

ghettos—city neighborhoods, especially slums, in which members of a minority group live because of social, economic, or legal pressure.

Ronald understood Dr. King's sense of urgency. Lately, it seemed that every time he watched TV, images of cities on fire filled the screen. During the mid-1960s, summer had become a season of racial violence, with rioting and the burning of buildings. Many African Americans had become impatient with the slow pace of reform. Some were even killed in battles with police and

Some young African-American civil rights leaders, such as Stokely Carmichael, turned away from King's strategy of nonviolence.

National Guard troops. Such a riot had occurred less than a month ago in Chicago.

Some young African-American civil rights leaders, such as **Stokely Carmichael**, turned away from King's strategy of nonviolence. Carmichael called for "Black Power." He believed that self-defense was more important than nonviolent protest. If necessary, blacks should carry guns while marching. Power was the only thing that was respected in the

---

People and Terms to Know

Stokely Carmichael—(1941–1998) African-American civil rights leader who coined the phrase "Black Power."

world. Another black leader, Malcolm X, had also declared that the days of nonviolence were over. But Dr. King refused to be swayed by such voices. He believed that nothing could be accomplished through violence.

When Chicago's mayor, Richard J. Daley, learned that King planned to lead a demonstration, he was outraged. After all, Chicago already had a slum-clearance program. Daley invited King to join in if he wanted to help. Meanwhile, Dr. King had rented an apartment on Chicago's West Side and moved in with his family. He wanted to observe firsthand what ghetto life was like.

This is what Dr. King learned: ghetto houses were often in terrible condition because landlords, known as "slumlords," failed to maintain their property. Crime was common because police tended to ignore lawlessness there. African Americans often paid higher rent than people living in white neighborhoods even though their apartments were in very poor condition. Some African Americans had good jobs. But they could not rent or buy a place in Chicago's white neighborhoods because white property owners refused their money. It was no wonder that African Americans felt trapped in the misery of the ghetto slums.

Dr. King had decided to focus on the issue of housing. That's why on August 5, Dr. King, Ronald Talbot, and 600 others marched through Marquette Park into a white neighborhood next to the ghetto. Among the marchers were members of several black gangs whom Dr. King had persuaded to give nonviolence a chance. There were also some whites

Martin Luther King, Jr. is helped after being struck by a rock during a civil rights march in Marquette Park.

who believed in justice. With Dr. King leading the way, they marched down narrow streets lined with hundreds of angry white residents screaming insults at them.

There was a police escort, but Ronald was frightened anyway. He had faced hostile crowds all over the South, but this seemed much worse. "Go back to Africa!" a woman shrieked.

With Dr. King leading the way, they marched down narrow streets lined with hundreds of angry white residents screaming insults at them.

As Ronald turned to see who had said this, another group of rocks rained down on the marchers. One policeman was hit by a rock. "I don't believe this!" he cried in amazement when he recognized the rock thrower as his next-door neighbor.

When the marchers reached a real estate office, Dr. King and those with him knelt in prayer. All around them, hundreds of whites were screaming. Someone threw a knife at Dr. King, but it missed. "I told you we should have called off the march," Ronald shouted. "We've got to get out of here, now!" With police help, the marchers made it back to the park, where the crowd of whites had grown.

Ronald noticed well-dressed women and men in business suits screaming hateful things.

The police helped the marchers into the waiting buses and cars. As Ronald reached for the bus door, an old man grabbed his arm, spun him around, and spit in his face. The man yelled, "I worked all my life for a house over here and no black is gonna get it!"

Mayor Daley and other white political and religious leaders in Chicago accused King of causing trouble.

Ronald pulled away in disgust and scrambled into the bus. He wiped his face as the bus started to move. Crowds of whites chased after the buses and cars, throwing rocks and smashing windows.

That evening, Ronald sat on a sofa in Martin Luther King's living room. Dr. King's wife Coretta and the four children were there. Dr. King talked about the march. "I've been in many demonstrations all across the South," he said, "but I can say that I have never seen—even in Mississippi and Alabama—mobs as hostile and as hate-filled as I've seen in Chicago."

Mayor Daley and other white political and religious leaders in Chicago accused King of causing trouble. They demanded that he call off plans for another march. King, however, told them that if they wanted him to stop marching, they would have to make justice a reality. So Daley called Dr. King to a meeting with the local labor and business leaders. They agreed that Chicago's Commission on Human Rights would make real estate agents post the city's open-housing policy—and the city *would* enforce it. Also, Chicago's banks agreed to lend money to qualified families regardless of race.

Dr. King said that he had proved that nonviolent protest worked in the North. But Ronald wasn't so sure. He thought about Dr. King's words as he traveled by bus back to Alabama. He couldn't help but think that in spite of their demonstration, it still might be a long time before justice became a reality in Chicago's West Side ghetto.

QUESTIONS TO CONSIDER

1. Why did Martin Luther King, Jr. want to lead a demonstration in Chicago?

2. In what way did Dr. King's views differ from those of other African-American civil rights leaders such as Stokely Carmichael and Malcolm X?

3. Why was Ronald frightened during the march?

4. Why do you think the demonstration brought out such angry reactions from many of Chicago's white people?

Oh Freedom! Kids Talk About the Civil Rights Movement with the People that Made it Happen
By Casey King, Linda Barrett Osborne, and Joe Brooks

In this book, several children interview family members, older friends, and neighbors about their recollections of the Civil Rights movement. Many of the adults played an active role in the movement and share their experiences here.

Martin Luther King, Jr. (Black Americans of Achievement)
By Robert E. Jakoubek and Nathan I. Huggins

This biography of King describes his life from his childhood to his death, including his attempt to bring the Civil Rights movement to the entire country.

Malcolm X
By Arnold Adoff and Rudy Gutierrez

Malcolm X had ideas that many people didn't like, but he also influenced large groups. This biography explains the events in his life as well as his beliefs.

A Changing
Society

Go For Broke!

BY DEE MASTERS

I voted for Senator Daniel K. Inouye. He's the U.S. senator who represents the state of Hawaii in Washington, D.C. Dan and I went through a lot together. We grew up in the same area. We were both Japanese Americans. And we both fought in the same Army army unit in World War II. But I voted against Dan once because I didn't understand Dan or myself.

Dan's story started in Yokohama, Japan, before either of us was born, when Dan's great-grandfather had some real bad luck. His house burned down, and so did two other homes. The law said that the person who lived in the house where the fire started had to pay for all the damage. The payment was $400. It doesn't sound like that much

Daniel Inouye served as a soldier in Italy during World War II.

today, but it seemed impossible then to the Inouye family. It was decided by Great-grandfather that his eldest son would go to Hawaii and work on the sugar plantations to pay the debt.

So Dan's grandfather went with his family and thousands of other poor Japanese men and women looking for a better life. My grandfather came to Hawaii at about the same time.

A lot of people would probably guess that once Dan's grandfather was away from Japan, maybe he wouldn't pay the debt. But he did. He worked hard in the sugarcane fields 12 to 14 hours a day. He got only $10 a month, but that was more than he would have earned in Japan. Now do you see why $400 was a lot of money? The family also started a simple version of a traditional Japanese bathhouse and charged for baths. It took them 20 years, but they paid off the debt.

Dan's family is proud of that accomplishment. They have lived with honor. I see that now, but I didn't see that when I first knew Dan.

Dan Inouye and I went to McKinley High in Hawaii. It was often called "Tokyo High" because nearly everyone who went there was of Japanese ancestry. Legally, there weren't supposed to be separate schools for Japanese Americans, but that's the way things worked out. To go to the better schools, you had to take a written and oral test. We did fine on the written test, but many students of Asian parents hadn't learned correct English pronunciation, so we failed the oral test.

"Why don't you wear shoes?" someone asked.

"Because I only have one pair," Dan answered.

At McKinley, I became a member of the honor society. Later, Dan was recommended for membership. To get in, he had to be interviewed by the student council.

"Why don't you wear shoes?" someone asked.

"Because I only have one pair," Dan answered. "They have to last."

"Why don't you wear a white shirt?"

"Why don't you wear a tie?"

"Are you going to answer?"

"Don't you care how you look?"

"What about your friends? They're **delinquents**!"

People and Terms to Know

delinquents—young people who cause trouble and sometimes break the law.

Then Dan got angry. "Because they don't wear shoes?" he cried. "Because they're poor?"

Dan stood up for himself and his friends. Time after time in his life, Dan Inouye stood up for people who couldn't speak for themselves. But I didn't see that in high school. To me, at the time, Dan just seemed like a troublemaker who made all us Japanese Americans look bad.

The big event that changed Daniel Inouye's life also changed the lives of almost everyone in the world. Dan was getting ready for church. Suddenly a voice announced over the radio: "This is no test! Pearl Harbor is being bombed by the Japanese!" It was December 7, 1941, and the bombing of the naval base at Pearl Harbor in Hawaii pulled the United States into World War II. You've maybe seen it in a movie. My mother cried when she looked up and saw the Japanese markings on the airplanes.

Dan had taken a Red Cross first aid course. Even while the bombs were dropping, he was called to help. He didn't come back for five days. Dan said that the kid who left home that morning "was lost forever in the debris of the war's first day, lost among the dead and the dying, and when I finally did come home, I was a 17-year-old man."

All Japanese Americans—whether we wore shoes and a white shirt or not—felt the hatred of other Americans who did not know us. Like most Japanese Americans, Dan worked hard to overcome the prejudice caused by the war. We were American!

All of us young Japanese Americans in Hawaii wanted to enlist, but at first we weren't allowed to. When we heard that we could enlist, Dan and most of our other classmates ran 3 miles to sign up. On that first day, 1,000 **Niseis** signed up. I was one, and proud of it.

Dan wasn't accepted at first because he was volunteering seventy-two hours a week at the Red Cross first aid station. This service was an important defense job. Dan was also studying to be a doctor at the university. Dan quit the Red Cross and the university to join the army.

The army tried to put him in the army band or use him as an interpreter. These were safer jobs than fighting as a soldier. But he stayed as a regular

---

People and Terms to Know

Niseis (NEE•sayz)—first generation of children of Japanese immigrants to be born in the United States.

soldier in the all-Nisei 442nd Regimental Combat Team. Our motto became "Go For Broke!" It meant give everything you could to everything you did. It helped us make it through the war, and after. I think that motto became Dan Inouye's personal motto.

Our motto became "Go For Broke!" It meant give everything you could to everything you did.

The 442nd fought in the <u>**European Theater**</u> of the war. There we saw how terrible war is for both soldiers and civilians. When we were in Italy at the end of the war, we saw civilians begging for army garbage because they didn't have anything else to eat. We saw parents selling children so they could feed the rest of their family. We watched men losing limbs—and sometimes their minds.

The lead man on one patrol was almost cut in two by machine gun fire as his patrol approached a small building. Dan's men threw grenades into the building. When they entered, there was one

People and Terms to Know

European Theater—area of fighting in World War II where the United States battled German and Italian forces—as opposed to the Pacific Theater, where the battles were against the Japanese.

German soldier barely alive. The German reached inside his uniform. Dan thought he was reaching for a gun and pumped three rifle shots into him. When Dan looked, the German soldier wasn't holding a gun. He was holding a picture of his wife and two children.

Dan never got used to killing. War hurts everyone, winners and losers, but today Dan makes it pretty clear that we have to support the men who lay their lives on the line for us. And he knows that from firsthand experience.

Dan came back from the war a captain and a hero. Our 442nd was the most decorated unit in the war. In his last engagement a few weeks before the end of the war, Dan's platoon was pinned down on a hill under machine gun fire. If something wasn't done quickly, they would all be picked off. Dan pulled the pin from a grenade. He stood up to throw it. Later he said he thought somebody punched him in the side, but we could see he had been shot in the stomach. He ran toward the machine gun nest and threw the grenade into it.

When the gun crew stumbled out, he cut them down with his **Tommy Gun**. Then, clutching his stomach where the blood was oozing out, he tossed two more grenades at a second gun. He fell to his knees and crawled up to the third gun. A German soldier stood up as Dan drew back to throw the last grenade. The German fired a rifle grenade at a range of 10 yards. The explosion smashed Dan's right elbow and just about tore off his arm. Then, a machine gun bullet hit him in the right leg. But Dan's grenade blew the last machine gun away.

A German soldier stood up as Dan drew back to throw the last grenade.

Days later the docs tried to save Dan Inouye's arm, but eventually it had to be **amputated**. But Dan came through. He learned to use his left arm. He finished college and went to law school. He got married. He was elected to the Hawaiian territorial government. After Hawaii became a state in 1959, Dan Inouye became a representative in Washington.

People and Terms to Know

Tommy Gun—nickname for Thompson submachine gun, an automatic weapon that was used by U.S. ground forces in World War II.

amputated—cut off in surgery.

Senator Inouye addresses the Democratic National Convention in 1968. His right sleeve is empty.

Eventually he became the first Japanese-American senator. He has been reelected six times.

I voted for him every time. When we were back in high school, though, I voted against him being in the honor society because he didn't wear shoes, a white shirt, or a tie. He wears them now, but that's not why I vote for him.

In 1962 when Dan was sworn into office, the House of Representatives was very still. It was about to witness the swearing in, not only of the first congressman from Hawaii, but also of the first Japanese American to serve in either house of Congress.

"Raise your right hand and repeat after me," said the officer to Dan.

The hush deepened as Dan raised not his right hand but his left and repeated the oath of office.

There was no right hand. It had been lost in World War II. One representative said that at that moment, a ton of prejudice slipped quietly to the floor of the House of Representatives.

Dan personally fought prejudice, poverty, and disability, and won for himself and others, including me. Thanks, Dan.

QUESTIONS TO CONSIDER

1. Why did the oldest son of the Inouye family move to Hawaii?

2. Why did the narrator once vote against Daniel Inouye?

3. Why did Japanese Americans have to overcome so much prejudice during World War II?

4. What did the "Go for Broke!" motto of the 442nd mean?

5. How was the 442nd different from other army units?

6. What examples of prejudice did Daniel Inouye face?

7. What do you think was meant by "a ton of prejudice slipped quietly to the floor of the House of Representatives" when Inouye was sworn in?

Viva La Huelga!

BY WALTER HAZEN

Police from the town of Delano stepped in and tried to stop us. But our leader, **Cesar Chavez**, told them that even if we had to wait a year right where we were, we would not turn back. And we didn't. Our destination was Sacramento, about 300 miles to the north of Delano. The year was 1966.

There were 77 of us marching in single file. We were all Mexican-American farm workers bound for California's capital. At the head of our column, one worker carried an American flag. A second marcher carried the flag of Mexico. A third carried the banner of the Virgin of Guadalupe, the patron

---

People and Terms to Know

Cesar Chavez—(1927–1993) Mexican-American labor leader. His efforts as head of the United Farm Workers Association led to better pay and working conditions for migrant workers.

U.F.W.O.C.

A.F.L.-C.I.O.

PICKET

Women stand on the picket line protesting against poor conditions for farm

saint of Mexico. Some workers carried homemade flags that read simply "huelga." *Huelga* is our Spanish word for "strike."

We marchers were members of the UFWA, the United Farm Workers Association. This was the union Cesar had formed in 1962. Its purpose was to see that **migrant workers** got higher pay and better working conditions. We had made some progress, but Cesar thought that a march on the capital was necessary to make people fully realize our problems.

On the first day of our march, we covered 21 miles. Poor Cesar! He'd been so busy planning the march that he'd paid little attention to his dress. His shoes fit poorly, and it showed that first night in the little town of Duroc. He had large blisters on the soles of both feet, and his left ankle was swollen to twice its size. But he didn't complain. He continued the march the following morning with the aid of a cane.

While we walked along the highway those first few days, my good friend Manuel and I chatted

---

People and Terms to Know

migrant workers—workers who travel from place to place picking and harvesting crops.

away. Mostly we talked about what had happened since the strike began six months earlier.

"Well," Manuel pointed out, "the owners of the **vineyards** have no one to blame but themselves for everything that's happened."

"These owners have grown rich while we've almost starved."

"That's for sure," I agreed. "Cesar always points out that the average income of migrant workers—only $1,500 a year—is well below the **poverty level** of $3,000! Geez—what a bunch of tightwads! These owners have grown rich while we've almost starved."

"Not only that," Manuel continued, "but think of the awful shacks we've been living in. There's no running water, and the temperatures are so hot inside you can hardly stand it."

"And what about the treatment we've put up with in the fields?" I added. "Remember old Dickson saying how lucky we are that he gives us drinking water?"

People and Terms to Know

vineyards—farms where grapes are grown on vines, either for food or to be used in making wine.

poverty level—dollar amount set by the U.S. government to determine the number of poor people in the country; the amount reflects the income received by a person or family in a year.

Manuel nodded. "And he sees nothing wrong with making us pay for it—and having all of us drinking out of the same old rusty cup!"

"Don't forget all the **pesticides**," I said. "Who knows how they're going to affect us on down the road. Man, I've been sprayed by those crop dusting planes so often I feel like a bug myself!"

And so we talked. So did the others. As for Cesar, he continued hobbling along on his bad feet. But his condition got worse. Soon his right leg was swollen to the knee. After a week he had to give it up and ride in a station wagon.

But no matter. Everywhere we stopped, we were greeted by fellow workers and sympathetic townspeople. They provided us with food, drink, and a place to stay for the night. At each stop we held a rally in a local park. Some people brought guitars and accordions, and we sang songs. At some stops, we had trouble getting to sleep because of the many questions people asked us.

People and Terms to Know

pesticides—chemicals used to kill insects that destroy crops.

"Do you think any of the vineyard owners will give in once you reach Sacramento?" an elderly worker asked me in Fresno.

"Let's hope so," I replied. "After all, people everywhere are helping us by boycotting grapes. Maybe the owners will listen after they see how much attention our march on the capital is getting."

On the ninth day of our journey, Cesar felt well enough to leave the station wagon and rejoin the march. He had to depend on his cane, but at least he was happy to be out walking with us again.

What made Cesar and all of us even happier were the crowds. The number of people who greeted us as we marched increased with each town. By the time we reached Stockton, just a short way from Sacramento, the "welcoming committee" had grown to 5,000. More and more people were throwing their support behind us.

The march was having its effect on at least one of the grape growers in the Delano area. That was Schenley Industries, Inc. While we were in Stockton, Cesar received a phone call from a Schenley representative. The representative told Cesar that his company was ready to sign an agreement with the union.

Cesar Chavez (center in front row) and others carried symbols of America, Catholicism, and Mexican-American culture in their protests.

Cesar hopped in a car at one o'clock in the morning and drove down to Los Angeles. After some discussion, an agreement was reached. Schenley officially recognized Cesar's union and agreed to give the grape pickers a pay raise of 35 cents an hour. It also agreed to make contributions to the UFWA's **credit union**.

Did Cesar take time to celebrate this important victory? No. He jumped back into the car and drove north to rejoin us on the march. Nine days later, we reached Sacramento. It was April 10, Easter Sunday, and it was raining. But this didn't stop 10,000 people from coming out to greet us.

It was April 10, Easter Sunday, and it was raining. But this didn't stop 10,000 people from coming out to greet us.

Cesar stood on the steps of the capitol building and told the happy crowd about the agreement with Schenley Industries. Everyone cheered. I didn't know it at the time, but I later learned that the agreement with Schenley was the first of its kind made with farm workers in America. Cesar and all of us had good reason to be proud.

I will never forget that march. Those 25 days brought us the national attention we needed. True, the contract Cesar got was with only one of

---

People and Terms to Know

credit union—association that makes loans to its members at low rates of interest.

the vineyard owners. There were many left who still refused to talk to us. But that one contract was a beginning.

*   *   *

Many of the conditions faced by migrant workers in the 1960s would not have been forced on them had they not been Mexican Americans. Much of society treated them like second-class citizens and did not expect them to stand up for themselves.

That's why the story of Cesar Chavez's work is important not just to the history of labor, but also to the history of civil rights. Cesar Chavez started the first successful farm workers union in U.S. history. In doing so, he built up Mexican-American pride and showed how peaceful methods of protest could change working conditions.

QUESTIONS TO CONSIDER

1. What was the purpose of the march from Delano to Sacramento?

2. What does the narrator have to say about the working conditions of California's grape pickers?

3. How did townspeople along the way greet the marchers?

4. Why was the agreement Cesar reached with Schenley Industries important?

Cesar Chavez (Hispanics of Achievement)
By Consuelo Rodriguez and Ruperto Garcia

This biography of Chavez highlights how he tried to overcome racism to gain success for himself and other workers.

An Elegy on the Death of Cesar Chavez
By Rudolfo A. Anaya and Gaspar Enriquez

Written in poetic form, this tribute to Chavez shows the love his supporters had for him. The book includes a biography and many photographs.

Farmworker's Friend:
The Story of Cesar Chavez
By David R. Collins

This extensive, thorough biography covers Chavez's entire life.

Remembering Wounded Knee

BY MARIANNE McCOMB

My friends and I used to think of a field trip as a day of freedom and fun. We were supposed to learn stuff, but mostly we talked and goofed around. But all that changed the day we took a field trip to **Wounded Knee**. It was that kind of trip. Wounded Knee affected us all.

Actually, Wounded Knee is a part of my personal history. My family lives maybe 50 miles from the **Pine Ridge Reservation** and always has. My

---

People and Terms to Know

Wounded Knee—place near Wounded Knee Creek on the Pine Ridge Indian Reservation in South Dakota where, in 1890, U.S. troops killed more than 300 unarmed men, women, and children. In 1973, it again became a scene of conflict.

Pine Ridge Reservation—land in southwestern South Dakota assigned in 1889 by the U.S. government to the Sioux. It is the second largest Indian reservation. (The first is the Navajo reservation in the Southwest.) Wounded Knee is in the Pine Ridge Reservation.

WE REMEMBER

1890– –1973

WOUNDED KNEE

Artist Bruce Carter's original woodcut links the battles at Wounded Knee in

grandmother likes to tell stories about what happened at Wounded Knee in 1973, and how some of the white people in town were angry with the Native Americans for laying **siege** to the place. But my grandmother wasn't angry. She says that the men and women who took over Wounded Knee were just protecting their rights. Before our field trip, I didn't understand what she meant by that. Now I do.

Sometimes he talks to school groups like ours because he wants kids to know the **truth.**

On the morning of the field trip, my teacher hustled us onto the bus. Before we knew it, we had arrived at Wounded Knee. Right away, a kind of tour guide came up to our bus. He told us his name was Black Hawk and that he was a part of the **Sioux** Nation. Sometimes he talks to school groups like ours because he wants kids to know the *truth*. Black

---

People and Terms to Know

siege—attempt by an army to force a city to surrender by surrounding it and cutting off supplies.

Sioux (SOO)—group of North American Indian tribes living in the Northern Plains area, such as the Dakotas and parts of Minnesota and Nebraska.

Hawk told us the story of the **massacre** at Wounded Knee in 1890. Here's what he said, as best as I can remember:

After 1830, the U.S. government began moving millions of Native Americans off their land and onto **reservations**. A large nation, the Lakota Sioux, moved onto the Pine Ridge Reservation. There was not enough good hunting land on the reservation, and the Sioux were worried they would starve.

Desperate, the Sioux held religious ceremonies to help the situation. This scared the whites who lived nearby. Federal troops were called in, and they forced the Sioux to stop. Some ran off and hid, but the soldiers found them. The Sioux had no choice but to surrender. That night, the whole group camped at Wounded Knee Creek. In the morning, as they prepared to move on, a small fight broke out. Someone got nervous and fired a shot. Then the soldiers went crazy and opened fire on all the Indians. They had an early type of machine gun and used the weapon even though the Indians were unarmed. No

---

People and Terms to Know

massacre (MAS•a•ker)—killing a group of people in an especially cruel way.

reservations—lands set aside by the government for a special purpose. During the 1800s, the U.S. government forced Native American nations east of the Mississippi to move west onto land they said would be "protected" from white settlers. Living conditions on these reservations continue to be harsh today.

Battle of Wounded Knee.

one's sure how many Indians were killed that day. Most people say that between 150 and 370 men, women, and children lost their lives.

The whole time Black Hawk was telling us this story, we were really quiet. I mean, we knew that the Indians had been treated badly in the past, but we had no idea that it was *this* bad. We didn't know that so many had been killed in cold blood.

Then a friend of mine said, "Hey, that's all ancient history. Nothing like that could happen today, right?"

"Wrong," Black Hawk said. Then he told us that the massacre at Wounded Knee was just *half* the story. Over the years, the Sioux and other Native American nations grieved for their murdered brothers and sisters. Life on the reservations continued to be harsh, and more and more land was stolen by whites.

Native American men and women became angrier and angrier. Why did the U.S. government put them on reservations and treat them like criminals? What gave it the *right*? This is what they asked themselves.

Native American leaders watched the Civil Rights movement of the 1960s with great interest. Many admired the way African Americans were fighting for their rights. They began telling themselves that they, too, should wage this kind of fight.

In 1968, a group of Native Americans formed a civil rights organization called the **American Indian Movement**. AIM held many protest events, includ-

People and Terms to Know

American Indian Movement—or AIM, organization started in 1968 with the goal of protecting Native American human rights. In the 1970s, AIM led several protest events to draw attention to the government's broken promises to American Indians.

ing some at the Washington, D.C., offices of the **Bureau of Indian Affairs**. Their purpose, AIM said, was to draw attention to the difficult lives of North American Indians.

The U.S. government wouldn't listen to AIM. In fact, it ignored every request that AIM made.

The U.S. government wouldn't listen to AIM. In fact, it ignored every request that AIM made. When AIM asked for a review of the promises the U.S. government had made to Native Americans, the government refused. When AIM demanded that 110 million acres of land be returned to Native Americans, the government ignored them. When AIM explained that they wanted protection for Indian religious and cultural freedom, the government basically said, "What for?"

So AIM decided it would have to make a stand. It would have to *show* the government and the American people that Native Americans would no longer be treated like second-class citizens. On

---

People and Terms to Know

Bureau of Indian Affairs—agency within the Interior Department in charge of reservations and relations between the government and Native American people.

February 27, 1973, about 200 members of AIM, led by **Dennis Banks** and **Russell Means**, met at Wounded Knee. They took the reservation village by force and renamed it, claiming that it was an independent nation. They would not leave Wounded Knee until the government promised a change in tribal leaders, a review of all treaties, and a Senate investigation into Native American issues.

Almost as soon as AIM took control of Wounded Knee, federal marshals moved in and a siege began. For ten weeks, the group of 200 Indians held firm at Wounded Knee. Each side made demands, but no agreement was reached. There were several gunfights. Two Indians were killed and a marshal was seriously injured.

Finally, on May 8, 1973, the siege ended. The Indians who had taken control of Wounded Knee were promised that their complaints would be investigated. Banks, Means, and the others surrendered.

People and Terms to Know

Dennis Banks—Anishinabe native born on Leech Lake Reservation in northern Minnesota, first national director of the American Indian Movement and one of the leaders of the 1973 siege at Wounded Knee. He continues to work for the protection of traditional Indian ways of life.

Russell Means—Lakota Sioux born in 1939 on Pine Ridge Reservation in southwestern South Dakota. He was a cofounder of the American Indian Movement and one of the leaders of the 1973 siege at Wounded Knee. He ran for president of the United States in 1988, exposed human rights violations in Nicaragua, and continues to work for the protection of human rights worldwide.

By the time Black Hawk finished his story, a couple of the kids were crying. I mean, it was all so awful and unfair. All these people wanted were the same rights that we took for granted every day.

From here on in, I promised myself, I would be brave like the men and women of AIM.

A couple of kids asked what happened after that. Did the government make good on its promises? Black Hawk explained that there was a lot of interest in Native American relations after Wounded Knee, but eventually it fizzled out. Also, the stress from Wounded Knee and other protests caused fighting within AIM itself. The national leadership fell apart in 1978. But, Black Hawk assured us, there are plenty of AIM chapters around the country that continue to work for Native American rights. They provide schools, health services, and counselling programs. They also work through the courts.

On the bus ride back to school, we were all quiet again. We had a lot to think about. Mostly I thought about the kind of courage it takes to really fight for your rights. From here on in, I promised myself, I would be brave like the men and women of AIM.

And like my grandmother and Black Hawk, I would work to make sure that Wounded Knee would not be forgotten.

QUESTIONS TO CONSIDER

1. What are your feelings about the 1890 massacre at Wounded Knee?

2. How was the 1973 siege at Wounded Knee similar to and different from the massacre?

3. What is AIM, and how was it involved in the siege?

4. In what ways does the narrator change as a result of the field trip to Wounded Knee?

Grandma in the 1960s

BY STEPHEN CURRIE

From: janthegreat@iloverocks.com
   To: linda.crowley@crowleyinc.com

Hi Grandma! How are things with you? I hope you gave everybody the day off. It's a great day for COLLECTING ROCKS (hint, hint, hint).

Anyway . . . I was wondering if you could help me with a school project (boring). It's for history (double boring). I have to find out what things were like for women a long time ago. So I asked you. :> (That's a grinning face in case you didn't know. Turn it sideways and you'll see.) Thanks!

Love ya, Jan

*   *   *